Diving & Snorkeling

Tahiti & French Polynesia

Jean-Bernard Carillet

Tony Wheeler

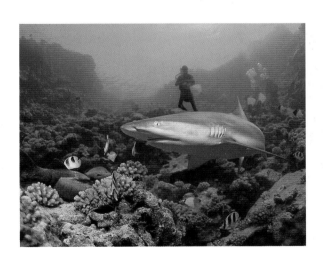

LONELY PLANET PUBLICATIONS
Melbourne • Oakland • London • Paris

Diving & Snorkeling Tahiti & French Polynesia
- A Lonely Planet Pisces Book

1st Edition – January 2001

Published by
Lonely Planet Publications
90 Maribyrnong St., Footscray, Victoria 3011, Australia

Other offices
150 Linden Street, Oakland, California 94607, USA
10a Spring Place, London NW5 3BH, UK
1 rue du Dahomey, 75011 Paris, France

Photographs
by photographers as indicated

Front cover photograph, by Philippe Bacchet
Shark and divers at La Faille, Manihi

Back cover photographs
Frogfish at Le Trou du Lagon, Tahiti, by Philippe Bacchet
Tropical refreshment, by Jean-Bernard Carillet
Diver and pufferfish at Toopua, Bora Bora, by
    Philippe Bacchet

Some of the images in this guide are available for
    licensing from **Lonely Planet Images**
email: lpi@lonelyplanet.com.au

ISBN 1 86450 071 9

text & maps © Lonely Planet
photographs © photographers as indicated 2001
dive site maps are Transverse Mercator projection

LONELY PLANET and the Lonely Planet logo are
trademarks of Lonely Planet Publications Pty Ltd.

Printed by H&Y Printing Ltd., Hong Kong

Contents

Authors

Jean-Bernard Carillet

After earning a degree in translation and in international relations from La Sorbonne Nouvelle in Paris, Jean-Bernard joined Lonely Planet's French office before becoming a full-time author. He has contributed to numerous travel guides, including *Marseilles*, *Corsica*, *South Pacific* and *Martinique, Dominique et Sainte-Lucie*. Diving instructor and incorrigible traveler, he will decamp at the slightest opportunity to travel, photograph and dive around the world. After several trips in Tahiti, he now considers French Polynesia a second home.

Tony Wheeler

Tony was born in England but grew up in Pakistan, the Bahamas and the U.S. He returned to England to study engineering, worked as an automotive design engineer, completed an MBA then set out with his wife, Maureen, on an Asian overland trip that ultimately led to them founding Lonely Planet in Australia in 1973. They have been traveling, writing and publishing guidebooks ever since. Tony took up diving as an interesting sideline to his travels and over the years has been diving from every continent except Antarctica. Diving in the warm waters of French Polynesia is always a pleasure, but Tony is a regular diver in the much cooler waters of Port Phillip Bay, near his home in Melbourne, Australia.

From the Authors

Jean-Bernard Carillet Thank you from the bottom of my heart to Yan, my faamu brother in Papeete, for his constant support and princely welcome. Heartfelt thanks to his family that has become mine. I'm also grateful to Patricia, to whom I owed my "home sweet home" welcome in Papeete.

This book would not have come to light without the cooperation of Hubert Clot, Henri and Josiane Pouliquen, Yves Lefèvre, Eric Le Borgne, Didier Forget, Serge Carcolse et Nathalie, Nicolas Castel, Didier Alpini, Anne et Michel Condesse, Thierry Paumel, Gilles Petre, Xavier Curvat and Marie, Bernard Blanc, Juan Pedro Lopez, Boubou, Ludovic Berne, Gilles Jugel, John Noonan, Miri Tatarata, Jean-Christophe Lapeyre and his friend, and Brigitte Vanizette. Thanks also to Corinne, Maria and Bruno for the wonderful time spent together.

My sincere thanks to the top-notch underwater photographers whose pictures enlighten this guide: Philippe Bacchet, so generous and so talented, Frédéric Di Meglio and Lionel Pozzoli, whose work appear in numerous dive magazines and exhibitions around the world.

Tony Wheeler My thanks go to Jonathan Ray and to the dive staff at Tahiti Plongée, Bathy's Club and Bora Bora Diving Centre, particularly to Henri, Juan-Pedro, Vincent, Michel and Anne and the other dive staff who made an English-speaking visitor feel perfectly at home.

Contributing Photographers

Many thanks to the photographers who contributed their images to this book: Philippe Bacchet, John Borthwick, Roslyn Bullas, Jean-Bernard Carillet, Frédéric Di Meglio, Michael McKay, Lionel Pozzoli, Tim Rock, Liz Thompson and Tony Wheeler.

From the Publisher

This long-awaited first edition was published in Lonely Planet's U.S. office. Roslyn Bullas, the Pisces publishing manager, braved the sharks and edited the text and photos with symbiotic assistance from editors Susan Charles Bush and David Lauterborn. Emily Douglas designed the cover and book with assistance from Ruth Askevold. Cartographer John Spelman, with help from Sara Nelson, Patrick Phelan, Ivy Feibelman and Angie Watts, created the maps under the supervision of Alex Guilbert. Lindsay Brown reviewed the Marine Life section for technical accuracy. Michael Lawrence contributed the sidebar on photographing sharks. Portions of the text were adapted from Lonely Planet's *Tahiti & French Polynesia*.

Pisces Pre-Dive Safety Guidelines

Before embarking on a scuba diving, skin diving or snorkeling trip, carefully consider the following to help ensure a safe and enjoyable experience:

- Possess a current diving certification card from a recognized scuba diving instructional agency (if scuba diving)
- Be sure you are healthy and feel comfortable diving
- Obtain reliable information about physical and environmental conditions at the dive site (e.g., from a reputable local dive operation)
- Be aware of local laws, regulations and etiquette about marine life and environment
- Dive at sites within your experience level; if possible, engage the services of a competent, professionally trained dive instructor or divemaster

Underwater conditions vary significantly from one region, or even site, to another. Seasonal changes can significantly alter site and dive conditions. These differences influence the way divers dress for a dive and what diving techniques they use.

There are special requirements for diving in any area, regardless of location. Before your dive, ask about environmental characteristics that can affect your diving and how trained local divers deal with these considerations.

Warning & Request

Things change—dive site conditions, regulations, topside information. Nothing stays the same for long. Your feedback on this book will be used to help update and improve the next edition. Excerpts from your correspondence may appear in *Planet Talk*, our quarterly newsletter, or *Comet*, our monthly email newsletter. Please let us know if you do not want your letter published or your name acknowledged.

Correspondence can be addressed to:
Lonely Planet Publications
Pisces Books
150 Linden Street
Oakland, CA 94607
email: pisces@lonelyplanet.com

Introduction

The scattered islands of French Polynesia are better known individually than collectively. The archipelago lies below the equator and east of the international date line, more or less directly south of the Hawaiian group and equidistant between Australia to the west and South America to the east. Though the name "French Polynesia" may not conjure many images, island names like Tahiti, Moorea, Bora Bora and Rangiroa have emotional resonance. Indeed, these islands are the epitome of the South Pacific dream: mountainous, lush green islands erupting from a deep blue sea, or low-lying atolls, a fragile necklace of sandy islets encircling a huge lagoon.

The Polynesian fantasy attracts a steady stream of visitors from Europe, the Americas and Australasia, who are drawn by the enticing images of paradise and who are willing to put up with the islands' reputation for wallet-emptying prices. The islands are often every bit as beautiful as the postcards promise, but visiting French Polynesia need not be quite such an attack on your bank balance. The scattering of super-luxury lagoon-side resorts are backed up by a substantial number of smaller hotels, local guesthouses and even backpacker hostels and campsites.

150°E	160°E	170°E	180°	170°W	160°W	150°W	140°W	130°W	

Tropic of Cancer

MEXICO

20°N

Hawaii (US)

International Date Line

PACIFIC OCEAN

10°N

Equator

10°S

PAPUA NEW GUINEA

FIJI

20°S

Tropic of Capricorn

AUSTRALIA

30°S

TAHITI & FRENCH POLYNESIA

NEW ZEALAND

40°S

The waters of French Polynesia are warm and clear, and the visibility usually ranges from excellent to unbelievable. The diving is always interesting and highly varied. Part of the Indo-Pacific coral reef system, the coral and marine life are similar to those seen across the Indian Ocean and the Pacific, from the Red Sea, down through Southeast Asia, around Australia and across the Pacific to Easter Island.

Around the high islands of the Society Group there are fine reefs, dense fish populations and special attractions ranging from manta rays in the Bora Bora lagoon to adrenaline-pumping shark-feeding excursions off Moorea.

The low-lying islands of the Tuamotus are classic atolls with narrow passes, where water courses in and out of the lagoons with each tidal change. Divers constitute a large part of the tourist flow to this island group, and the opportunity to dive with the sharks at Rangiroa has made this particular island one of the best-known dive sites in the Pacific.

Far fewer divers continue beyond the Tuamotus to the Marquesas, where the visibility may not be as spectacular or the dive conditions as textbook perfect. But the opportunity to dive, or even simply snorkel, with huge groups of electra dolphins and other pelagics is unmatched.

Finally, very few visitors, and even fewer divers, make it south to the Austral Group—even though the island of Rurutu is among the best places in the world to dive with humpback whales.

This book provides information on nearly 50 of the best dives in French Polynesia, divided according to island group. Information about location, depth range, access and expertise rating is given for each site. You will also find detailed descriptions of each site, outlining conditions and noting topographical features and marine life you can expect to see. The Marine Life section provides a gallery of French Polynesia's common vertebrate and invertebrate marine life. Though this book is not intended to be a stand-alone travel guide, the Overview and Practicalities sections offer useful information about the islands, while the Activities & Attractions section offers ideas on how to spend your time above the water.

ROSLYN BULLAS
French Polynesia's natural beauty entices visitors to its shores.

Overview

French Polynesia consists of five island groups spread across the blue waters of the South Pacific. They cover more than 2,000km (1,200 miles) from east to west and nearly as far from north to south. The Society Islands are the best known of the groups, containing most of French Polynesia's population and the only international airport. The group includes Tahiti, quite possibly the most familiar and most magical island name in the whole Pacific,

JEAN-BERNARD CARILLET

and Bora Bora, arguably the most beautiful island in the Pacific.

To the east are the scattered, low-lying Tuamotus, known to early European navigators as the "dangerous islands." The small Gambier Archipelago is an isolated outlier at the southeastern end of the group. Farther northeast are the remote and brooding Marquesas islands, made famous by writer Herman Melville, painter Paul Gauguin and singer Jacques Brel. Far south of the Society and Tuamotu Groups is the long chain of the Australs.

The islands' total population is roughly 220,000. About 86% of the populace lives in the Society Group, and about 40% of that in Papeete, the capital city of Tahiti. The people are predominantly Polynesian, descendants of the expert navigators who populated the eastern half of the South Pacific, paddling their mighty canoes as far north as Hawaii, as far east as Easter Island and as far south as New Zealand. As the name indicates, French Polynesia is a colony of France and treated like a far-flung province

JEAN-BERNARD CARILLET

Moorea's Mt. Rotui offers sweeping views.

of "metropolitan" France. There is a small French population, with their fingers on the government and economic pulses. Other smaller groups include Chinese, who control much of the business and trading life of the colony, and *demis*, who are part Polynesian, part Chinese or French.

French Polynesia's economy is far from balanced—imports far exceed exports. Financial transfers from France help in coping with the shortfall. Black pearls, tourism and fishing are the country's biggest industries.

History

Huge volcanic eruptions created the islands of Polynesia between 1 and 3 million years ago. Human settlement came much later; the islands of Polynesia and New Zealand were the last places on earth to be settled by humans. Polynesia—meaning "many islands"—stretches from Tonga in the west through the Cook Islands and French Polynesia to the small Pitcairn Group in the southeast. The Polynesian people, linked by a common language and an ancestry that can be traced back to the great migration voyages that populated the Pacific, include the native Hawaiians of the U.S. state of Hawaii and the Maori people of New Zealand.

The populating of the Pacific took place in a number of successive waves, moving eastward across the Pacific from Southeast Asia. Anthropologists and archaeologists believe that a great population movement took place from around the start of the Christian era to AD 300, moving on from Fiji, Tonga and Samoa to the islands of French Polynesia. This movement settled the Marquesas, completely overshooting the Society Islands and the Tuamotus. Another 500 years passed before the next migration wave, starting from the Marquesas, moved north to the Hawaiian Islands, southeast to Easter Island and southwest to the Society

JEAN-BERNARD CARILLET

Ancient Polynesian culture all but vanished in the wake of European colonial expansion.

JEAN-BERNARD CARILLET

Shipborne explorers left their mark over centuries of contact and conquest.

Islands. It was only 1,000 years ago that the last migration wave, starting from the Society Islands, moved on to the Cook Islands and finally to New Zealand.

European contact with the islands of modern-day French Polynesia commenced with Portuguese, Spanish, Dutch and English explorers who, in the course of great voyages across the Pacific, chanced upon various islands in the Polynesian region.

It was the arrival of Englishman Samuel Wallis, whose ship HMS *Dolphin* eased into the Tahiti lagoon in 1767, that really kicked off the European fascination with Polynesia. He was followed only months later by the French explorer Louis Antoine de Bougainville. These two pioneers brought back tales of beautiful islands, noble savages and Venus-like women with "the celestial form of that goddess," fueling a myth that has persisted to the present day.

One year later, in 1768, Captain Cook turned up in the *Endeavour* en route to his pioneering visits to New Zealand and Australia. Ten years were to pass before the next visitors, when Captain William Bligh turned up with the HMS *Bounty*. The *Bounty* had come to Tahiti to collect breadfruit seedlings, which the British intended to feed their slave populations in the Caribbean. The ensuing mutiny, led by the *Bounty*'s midshipman Fletcher Christian, imprinted the Tahitian myth even more firmly into the western mind.

Nudity, flowers in the hair, lascivious dancing, tattoos and indiscriminate sex were all part of that myth. Hardly surprisingly, the missionaries soon turned up, intent upon stamping out all that activity. Alcohol, European-borne diseases, European weapons and a wholesale assault on Polynesian culture by a motley crew of whalers, traders and missionaries soon sent the Polynesian population plummeting. The Pomare family of Tahiti, particularly under Queen Pomare V, who reigned from 1827-1877, made some progress in uniting the individual islands, but the European powers were busy snatching up any unclaimed patch of land during their great colonial expansion.

In 1842 the French took over Tahiti, kicking out the Protestant missionaries who had effectively formed a proxy English government. It took the rest of the century for French control to extend throughout the island groups, and it was not until the 20th century that the Polynesian population decline was arrested. French Polynesia remained remote and little visited through the first half of the 20th century, although visits by writers and artists—most notably painter Paul Gauguin, who died on Hiva Oa in the Marquesas in 1903—nurtured the Polynesian myth.

During WWI there were a couple of colorful naval incidents in French Polynesian waters, and a German ship shelled Papeete on one occasion, but after the war the islands returned to their peaceful existence. WWII touched the islands only peripherally, although a large U.S. air base on Bora Bora certainly had its effects. After the war, modern tourism brought larger numbers of visitors to the region.

The opening of a modern international airport on Tahiti in 1961, fast jet services across the Pacific, the filming of Marlon Brando's version of *Mutiny on the Bounty* and the commencement of French nuclear testing on Moruroa atoll in the Tuamotus all combined to hurl French Polynesia into the modern age. Fortunately, nuclear testing is permanently halted, but tourism—and scuba diving—is playing an ever more important role in the islands' economies.

Geography

French Polynesia's five distinctly different island groups include almost every type of island found in the Pacific. The Society Islands are mainly mountainous high islands with beautiful lagoons protected by barrier reefs, sometimes dotted with small fringing islands known as *motu*. Furthermore, the Society Group is subdivided into the Leeward (westernmost) and Windward (easternmost) Islands. The Tuamotus, classic low-lying coral atolls, include islands famed for scuba diving. They also include one high island, Makatea, a textbook example of the upthrust coral reef. The Gambier Archipelago, at the tail end of the Tuamotus, is a small group of predominantly high islands in a single large lagoon.

The remote Marquesas are rugged high islands devoid of lagoons and barrier reefs, where Herman Melville launched his literary career and Gauguin painted his most famous South Seas visions. Finally, there are the even more remote and scattered Australs, predominantly high islands, though not as high as the Society Group or the Marquesas.

The highest point in French Polynesia is Mt. Orohena at 2,241m (7,350ft), on Tahiti.

High Island, Low Island or Makatea?

French Polynesia has essentially three island types: high island, low island and makatea. You will find diving at all of them.

High Islands Cloaked in dense green vegetation and rising precipitously from the sea, the mountainous volcanic islands of French Polynesia are familiar scenes from Pacific postcards and calendars. Most of the islands of the Society Group are high islands, including Tahiti, Moorea, Huahine, Raiatea, Tahaa and Bora Bora. They're also the six Society Islands with scuba diving operations. All of these islands are surrounded by shallow lagoons, often with an outlying barrier reef fringed by small sandy motu. The high islands of the Society Group are generally volcanic in origin but they can also be the result of geologic upheaval.

The islands of the Marquesas are also high islands, but there is no barrier reef or protected lagoon; the open ocean washes straight up to the shores of these islands.

JEAN-BERNARD CARILLET
Volcanic activity shaped the region's high islands.

Low Islands With one exception, all the islands of the Tuamotus are classic low-lying coral atolls, where a narrow barrier reef surrounds a shallow lagoon. The outer islands around this reef are low-lying, typically rising no more than 3 to 5m (10 to 15ft) above sea level. The narrow entrances into the lagoon are often too shallow or restricted to allow ships to enter. These lagoon entrances are known as passes. At high tide, or when there's a large swell, water may flood across even more restricted channels known as *hoa*. The lagoons of the Tuamotu islands vary from just a kilometer or two across to huge reef-encircled seas such as the Rangiroa lagoon, which stretches 75km (46 miles) east to west and 25km (15 miles) north to south.

JEAN-BERNARD CARILLET
Atolls typify the Tuamotu archipelago.

Makatea Apart from one atoll, the islands of the remote Austral Group are all high islands, some (Raivavae and Tubuai, for example) have sheltered lagoons like the high islands of the Society Group, while others (like Rapa) tumble straight into the deep ocean like the high islands of the Marquesas. Rurutu, however, the only island in the Austral Group with scuba diving facilities, is a *makatea* island. This term refers to a coral island that at some point has been thrust up above sea level by a geologic disturbance. Rurutu is a textbook example of this type of island.

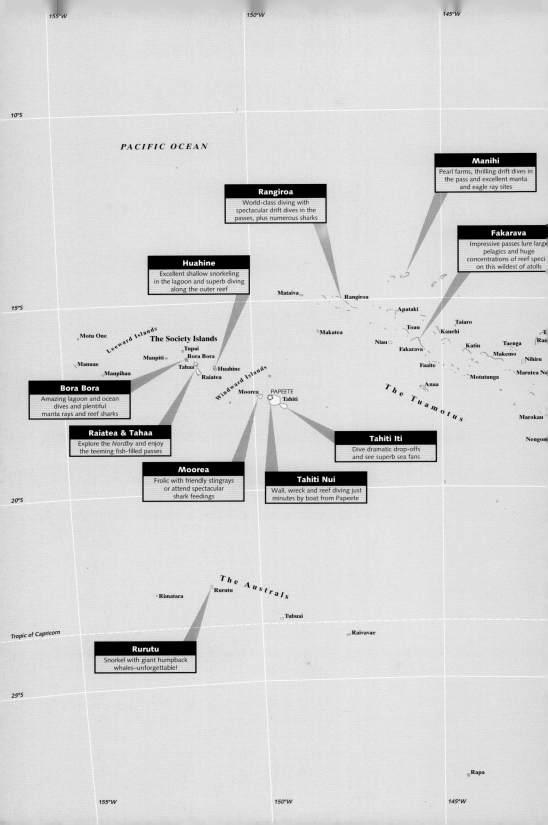

155°W   150°W   145°W

10°S

PACIFIC OCEAN

Manihi
Pearl farms, thrilling drift dives in the pass and excellent manta and eagle ray sites

Rangiroa
World-class diving with spectacular drift dives in the passes, plus numerous sharks

Fakarava
Impressive passes lure large pelagics and huge concentrations of reef speci on this wildest of atolls

Huahine
Excellent shallow snorkeling in the lagoon and superb diving along the outer reef

Mataiva

Rangiroa

15°S

Motu One

Leeward Islands

The Society Islands

Tupai
Bora Bora

Maupiti

Manuae

Maupihaa

Tahaa

Huahine

Raiatea

Makatea

Apataki

Toau

Niau

Fakarava

Faaite

Anaa

Taiaro

Kauehi

Katiu

Taenga

Makemo

Motutunga

Marutea Ne

Nihiru

The Tuamotus

Marokau

Nengon

Bora Bora
Amazing lagoon and ocean dives and plentiful manta rays and reef sharks

Windward Islands

Moorea

PAPEETE
Tahiti

Raiatea & Tahaa
Explore the *Nordby* and enjoy the teeming fish-filled passes

Tahiti Iti
Dive dramatic drop-offs and see superb sea fans

Moorea
Frolic with friendly stingrays or attend spectacular shark feedings

Tahiti Nui
Wall, wreck and reef diving just minutes by boat from Papeete

20°S

The Australs

Rimatara

Rurutu

Tubuai

Raivavae

Tropic of Capricorn

Rurutu
Snorkel with giant humpback whales–unforgettable!

25°S

Rapa

155°W   150°W   145°W

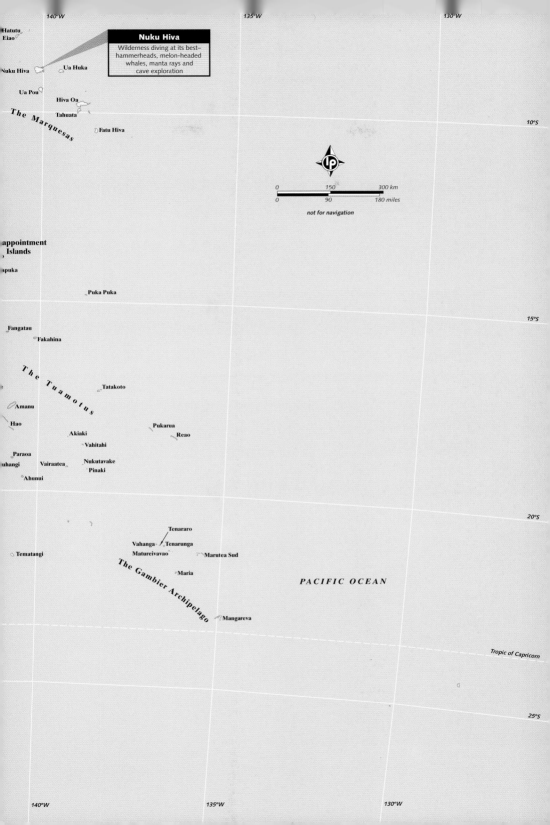

140°W   135°W   130°W

Hatutu
Eiao

Nuku Hiva   Ua Huka

Nuku Hiva
Wilderness diving at its best–
hammerheads, melon-headed
whales, manta rays and
cave exploration

Ua Pou   Hiva Oa
     Tahuata

The Marquesas   Fatu Hiva

10°S

0   150   300 km
0   90   180 miles

not for navigation

appointment
Islands

apuka

Puka Puka

15°S

Fangatau
   Fakahina

The Tuamotus

Tatakoto

Amanu

Hao

   Akiaki   Pukarua
          Reao
   Vahitahi

Paraoa
uhangi   Vairaatea   Nukutavake
         Pinaki
  Ahunui

20°S

        Tenararo
   Vahanga / Tenarunga
Tematangi   Matureivavao   Marutea Sud

The Gambier Archipelago   Maria

PACIFIC OCEAN

     Mangareva

Tropic of Capricorn

25°S

140°W   135°W   130°W

LIZ THOMPSON

Practicalities

Climate

French Polynesia has two distinct seasons: the wet season, from November to April, and the dry season, from May to October. February and March are the hottest and most humid months, with brief violent storms bringing heavy rainfall. Rain is rare during the dry season, and temperatures are slightly cooler, although the temperatures are rarely impossibly high and do not vary a great deal throughout the year. The air temperature rarely gets much above 30°C (mid 80°F) or drops as low as 20°C (70°F). The water temperature is comfortably constant between 26 and 29°C (79 and 84°F) year-round. The dry season brings better dive conditions and often superb visibility, although conditions are generally excellent most of the year.

In the Marquesas, July and August are the wettest months, while the Australs, well to the south, tend to be slightly wetter and rather cooler than the other islands. In winter, air temperatures in the Australs can fall to as low as 10°C (50°F).

Language

Tahitian and French are the official languages of French Polynesia, although Tahitian is spoken much more than it is written. Much of the tourist industry uses English but if you get off the beaten track, it is definitely useful to know some French. Fortunately, you won't be ignored because of your accent—bad French is readily accepted in French Polynesia!

JEAN-BERNARD CARILLET
A fisherman sells his day's catch in Tahiti Iti.

Tahitian, known as *Maohi*, belongs to the linguistic group of Polynesian languages that includes Samoan, Maori, Hawaiian, Rarotongan and Tongan. There are many dialects of Tahitian, including the Tuamotan or Paumotan dialect of the Tuamotus and the Marquesan dialect of the Marquesas, but it was the spread of Christianity through French Polynesia in the 19th century that helped to make Tahitian, the dialect spoken on Tahiti, the most widespread dialect.

Few Tahitian words have managed to make their way into English or any other languages. The two familiar exceptions are "tattoo" from the Tahitian *tatau* and "taboo" from the Tahitian *tapu* or *tabu*.

Getting There

The vast majority of visitors arrive by air at the one international airport, Tahiti Faaa. Three French airlines—Air France, Corsair and AOM—fly to Tahiti from France via the U.S. West Coast. Hawaiian Airlines is the only U.S. airline to operate to Tahiti, with connections from Hawaii. Qantas Airways connects Tahiti with Australia, and the Tahitian airline Air Tahiti Nui has connections with Japan and the U.S. West Coast. Aircalin, the New Caledonian airline, connects Tahiti with the other French Pacific colonies, Wallis and Futuna and New Caledonia, and with Fiji, with onward connections to Australia.

The most comprehensive links with Tahiti are operated by Air New Zealand, which has connections from Europe via Los Angeles to Tahiti and on to the Cook Islands, Fiji, New Zealand and Australia.

French Polynesia is a popular stopping point for trans-Pacific yachts and a handful of adventure-cruise ships that come through the islands.

French Diving Terms & Common Marine Life

Most dive centers are used to dealing with English speakers, but it is always worth knowing where to look when a fellow diver says you have dropped your *palmes*, your *ceinture* looks loose, and watch out for the *requin*:

a beginner: un débutant	**clam:** bénitier
a beginner's dive or first dive: un baptême	**coral:** coraux
a dive: une plongée	**grouper:** mérou céleste
a dive center: un centre de plongée	**jellyfish:** meduse
a dive course: une formation	**lobster:** langouste
a diver: un plongeur, une plongeuse	**Moorish idol:** poisson cocher
a divemaster: un moniteur	**moray eel:** murène javanaise
a diving license or C-card: un brevet de plongée	**parrotfish:** poisson perroquet
a drift dive: une plongée à la dérive	**reef:** récif
an experienced diver: un confirmé	**sea star:** étoile de mer
air tanks: des bouteilles de plongée	**shark:** requin
BC (buoyancy compensator): gilet de sécurité, stab	**stingray:** raie pastenague
depth gauge: profondimètre	
dive computer: un ordinateur de plongée	
fins: des palmes	
mask: un masque	
regulator: un détendeur	
snorkel: un tuba	
snorkeling: plongée sans bouteille	
wetsuit: une combinaison de plongée	
weight belt: une ceinture de plombs	

Gateway City – Papeete

With a population of more than 100,000, Papeete, the capital of Tahiti, is by far the largest center in French Polynesia. It is also the government and business center of the islands and the site of the only international airport, 6km (4 miles) west of downtown, in Faaa suburb. Although Papeete has almost totally lost its easygoing South Seas charm, it's still a fascinating port city with a bustling waterfront crowded with visiting yachts, French navy vessels, inter-island cargo ships, high-speed passenger catamarans and passenger ships and even the odd cruise ship.

JEAN-BERNARD CARILLET
Papeete boasts a bustling waterfront.

Tahiti has a variety of attractions, ranging from museums to four-wheel-drive excursions into the mountainous interior, but despite its seductive name, it's not the main tourist center of French Polynesia. From the tourist's point of view, it's not the main dive center, either, though the island has a number of dive operators and some fine dive sites. In fact, Tahiti's main function is as a jumping-off point for the

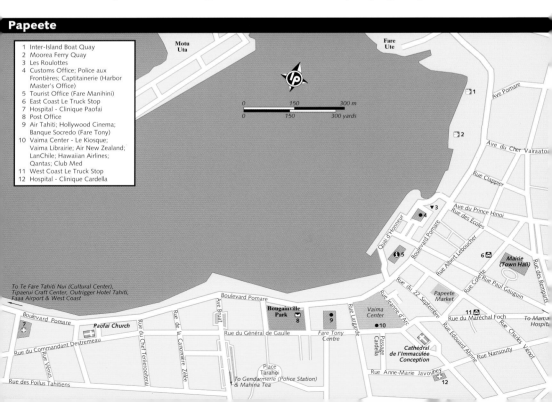

Papeete

1 Inter-Island Boat Quay
2 Moorea Ferry Quay
3 Les Roulottes
4 Customs Office; Police aux Frontières; Captitainerie (Harbor Master's Office)
5 Tourist Office (Fare Manihini)
6 East Coast Le Truck Stop
7 Hospital - Clinique Paofai
8 Post Office
9 Air Tahiti; Hollywood Cinema; Banque Socredo (Fare Tony)
10 Vaima Center - Le Kiosque; Vaima Librairie; Air New Zealand; LanChile; Hawaiian Airlines; Qantas; Club Med
11 West Coast Le Truck Stop
12 Hospital - Clinique Cardella

other islands. Flights and shipping services all fan out from Tahiti, and a variety of hotels and French Polynesia's best restaurants ensure that a stop in Papeete is a relatively painless experience.

Getting Around

The principal domestic airline is Air Tahiti (weekdays: ☎ 86 40 00 or ☎ 86 42 42; weekends: ☎ 86 41 84 or ☎ 86 41 95) with connections to all the major islands in the Society Group and to important centers in all the other island groups. Most services connect through Tahiti, although there is a direct connection between Bora Bora in the Society Group and Rangiroa in the Tuamotus, both popular scuba diving destinations.

Air Moorea (☎86 41 41) operates a shuttle service between Tahiti and the neighboring island of Moorea, a flight that takes less than 10 minutes. There are a variety of passenger and car ferries operating between Tahiti and Moorea, with the fastest services taking about half an hour. The fast passenger ship *Ono-Ono* (☎ 45 35 35) runs from Tahiti to Huahine, Raiatea, Tahaa and Bora Bora in the Society Group several times a week. Slower and less frequent services ply the islands in other groups, including the popular cargo-cruise ship *Aranui*.

Le Truck

Le truck is the public bus service of French Polynesia. The vehicles are just what the name indicates: trucks. Down each side of the back is a bench seat for passengers. Riding le truck is something every visitor to French Polynesia should do. You'll enjoy natural air-conditioning (the breeze blows straight through) and convivial fellow passengers.

Unfortunately, only Tahiti has a reasonably comprehensive and regular le truck service. Note that you pay at the end of the trip and that for many routes there is a set fare, irrespective of distance.

Moorea has a fairly regular le truck route around the island plus services for ferry arrivals and departures. Bora Bora has le trucks connecting the major hotel enclave with boat and flight arrival and departure points. On some other islands there are even more-limited services. On Raiatea and Huahine there are just a couple of services a day between outlying villages and the main town. Tahaa and Maupiti have no regular le truck service.

There are hardly any roads in the Tuamotus and in the Marquesas, and the only le trucks in Taiohae (Nuku Hiva) and Atuona (Hiva Oa) are those reserved for school transport. There is virtually no public transport in the Australs.

JEAN-BERNARD CARILLET

Only on Tahiti is there a reasonably reliable public transportation service. On other islands renting a car, motor scooter or bicycle is the most reliable way of getting around. It's usually possible to charter boats on the island lagoons.

Entry

Except for French citizens, anyone visiting French Polynesia needs a passport, and the regulations are much the same as for France itself; if you need a visa to visit France, then you will need one to visit French Polynesia. Anyone from a European Union (EU) country can stay for up to three months without a visa. So can Australians and citizens of a number of other European countries, including Switzerland.

Citizens of Argentina, Canada, Chile, Japan, Mexico, New Zealand, the U.S. and some other European countries can stay for up to one month without a visa. Other nationalities need a visa, which can be applied for at French diplomatic missions. Visa regulations for French Polynesia can change on short notice, so visitors should check with a French diplomatic office or their travel agent shortly before traveling.

Apart from permanent residents and French citizens, any visitor to French Polynesia must have an onward or return ticket. Visitors arriving from Fiji or from Pago Pago in American Samoa must have their baggage fumigated upon arrival.

Money

The unit of currency in French Polynesia is the franc CFP (*cours du franc Pacifique*), or CFP, whose value is tied to the French franc (and Euro). There are three major banks operating in French Polynesia, of which Banque Socredo has the most branches. On the main islands in the Society Group there are ATMs (DABs, or *distributeurs automatiques de billets,* in French) that will give you cash advances on your Visa or MasterCard or, if linked to the international Cirrus or Maestro networks, will let you withdraw money straight from your home bank account. Note that there is a weekly limit of 35,000 CFP for ATM withdrawals or advances from any one account.

There are hefty bank charges for changing money or traveler's checks in

JEAN-BERNARD CARILLET
Drums accompany traditional dances.

French Polynesia. Expensive and middle-range hotels and restaurants on the tourist islands, souvenir and jewelry shops, dive centers, the major supermarkets and Air Tahiti all accept credit cards.

Tipping is not expected in French Polynesia, and except for black pearls and similar expensive jewelry or craftwork sold directly by the artist, bargaining is not practiced.

Time

French Polynesia is east of the international date line and is 10 hours behind GMT. When it's noon in Tahiti, it is 2pm in San Francisco, 11pm in Paris and 8am the next day in Sydney. The Marquesas are a half-hour ahead of the rest of French Polynesia (noon in Tahiti is 12:30pm in the Marquesas). Daylight saving time is not observed in French Polynesia.

Electricity

The electricity is usually 220V and operates on a 24-hour basis on all the major islands. Sockets are generally the European two round pin style. Some deluxe establishments may also provide 110V supply for Americans and Japanese.

Weights & Measures

The metric system is standard in French Polynesia. In this book, both metric and imperial measurements are given, except for specific references to depth in the dive site sections, which are given in meters only.

What to Bring

Topside

The climate is mild and dress rules are relaxed, so you don't need to bring much with you. Coats and ties are not required except on the most formal business occasions, and it would take a cold day in the Australs, the most southerly islands of the group, to need more than a short-sleeved shirt or blouse. Shorts, swimsuits and lightweight cotton clothes are the order of the day.

This is the tropics, and visitors should be prepared for the intense sun (bring sunscreen, sunglasses and a hat), while not forgetting that heavy (but usually short) downpours are not at all uncommon. The temperatures will remain high, however, so an umbrella is probably wiser than a raincoat. Insect repellent can be near vital, particularly if you have any sensitivity to mosquito bites, and a small first-aid kit is always wise. Plastic shoes or an old pair of sneakers are useful for avoiding cuts when walking on dead coral. To keep your camera gear protected from water and humidity, bring a plastic bag and desiccant packets.

Imported goods are always expensive in French Polynesia. Bring sunscreen, film, toiletries and any other consumables with you from home. If, however, you find you need a swimsuit or a new T-shirt, there are plenty for sale, often at not-too-excessive prices; such items are imported from Europe, the U.S. and Asia.

Laundromats are very rare outside of Papeete, where they are expensive. Unless you are staying at an upscale hotel or resort, be prepared to wash your own clothes. The official baggage weight limit on Air Tahiti flights is just 20kg (44lbs) for overseas visitors, so pack light.

Dive-Related Equipment

In the Society Islands, the Tuamotus and the Marquesas, the water temperatures will always be warm. The water temperatures at Rurutu, well to the south, will be cooler. A lightweight short wetsuit (3mm) is all that is needed, and most divers will be quite happy wearing just a lycra skin to protect from coral scratches, or even just a swimsuit and T-shirt.

Equipment rentals and dive trip costs are in line with most international dive destinations, but the condition and age of dive equipment is highly variable. At the more upscale tourist-oriented dive operators, the equipment is new, high quality and in excellent condition. This may not always be the case at low-key dive operators. Some operators only provide a pressure gauge, no depth gauge, for example. The situation may be even worse with dive operators on Tahiti island, who principally cater to local French expatriates, not tourists. Since these divers generally have their own equipment, the rental equipment may be very old and worn. Bringing your own equipment may be worthwhile in French Polynesia. If you do need to buy diving equipment, **Nautisports** in the Fare District of Papeete is your best bet (see the Listings section for details).

Certified divers will need to show their dive card, and it's a good idea to have your dive logbook with you. Dive centers accept any dive association accreditation (PADI, NASDS, etc., although the main French qualification is CMAS), but they may ask you to do a preliminary dive to check your expertise. A medical certificate is necessary if you are participating in a dive course. In France itself you must have a current medical certificate for any diving, and it is always possible that the less tourist-oriented dive operators may ask for a certificate. No certification is required for supervised beginners' dives—*baptême*, as they are known— although parental authorization is required for minors.

Underwater Photography

The lack of plankton guarantees maximum water clarity. For beginners, a disposable camera will suffice, but these are waterproof only to 3 or 4m (10 to 13ft).

Divers with high-performance equipment should check that the charger and pins are compatible before plugging in the flash. Film processing services, camera sales and repair services are available in Papeete. The most reputable dealers include **Photo Tahiti** in Vaima Center (☎ 42 97 34), **QSS**, also in Vaima Center (☎ 50 85 85) and **Polydis-Photo Service**, 17 rue du Régent, Paraita (☎ 42 82 82). Camera and lens rentals are not commonly available in French Polynesia, though dive centers may sometimes provide this service for visiting divers.

Business Hours

Shops and offices are normally open from 7:30 or 8am to 5pm weekdays, although many places close an hour earlier on Friday afternoon. A long and leisurely lunch break is still common, though many places now tend to work straight through the day. Some food shops and supermarkets remain open late in the evening.

On the weekends, shops are generally open Saturday morning but closed Saturday afternoon, and almost all are closed on Sunday. Food shops and supermarkets are the exception. Even on the smaller islands they tend to stay open seven days a week.

Accommodations

French Polynesia is famous for its sumptuous over-water bungalows, but you'll also find everything from camping and hostels all the way up to 5-star luxury hotels and resorts. The largest and greatest variety of accommodations are found on the most touristy islands, particularly Tahiti, Moorea, Bora Bora and Rangiroa. Nevertheless, accommodations in French Polynesia are generally costly. Some of the most luxurious hotels are located on the motu, which are noted for their fine beaches.

Not all expensive places have air-conditioning, but sea breezes make this a pleasure rather than a discomfort. Check to see if credit cards are accepted. They will be at the luxury resorts, but a surprising number of middle-range places

JEAN-BERNARD CARILLET

French Polynesia has no shortage of luxury resorts.

accept only cash. There is generally an 8% government tax on the mid-range and top-end places.

Staying with a family in a guesthouse, or "pension," is popular on nearly every island and may be the only option on more remote islands. This kind of accommodation can mean a room in the family house or an independent bungalow. On the more remote islands, standards can be fairly basic.

Dining & Food

You will eat well in French Polynesia. You'll find a wide variety of western cuisine and some strong French influence, sometimes tantalizingly combined with Polynesian ingredients and recipes. *Poisson cru*, the local raw fish dish, is a firm favorite. Snacks and light meals include hamburgers and pizzas, but the best budget food choices are the excellent sandwiches made with French-style baguettes.

The other bargain-priced dining possibility is the *roulottes*, vans with kitchens inside and a fold-down counter along each side for their customers. The nightly gathering of roulottes by the quayside in Papeete is a real institution.

Most restaurants are concentrated in the Papeete area and on the main islands. They serve French, Polynesian and Chinese specialties. It is worth trying a buffet dinner and Polynesian dance performance at one of the luxury resorts. On remote islands, eating at your guesthouse may be the only choice available, and the diet may be predominantly fish and rice. Of course, the seafood is fresh and excellent even if the variety is relatively limited.

On the bigger islands, the markets are laden with food, vegetables, fruit, meat and fish. There are well-equipped supermarkets on these islands and small stores almost everywhere. Drinks include delicious fresh fruit juices, coconut water and

Roadside *roulottes* are a bargain dining tradition along the quayside in Papeete.

locally produced and imported mineral waters. With the exception of Papeete and Bora Bora, it is not advisable to drink the tap water in French Polynesia. Hinano is the excellent local beer, and the French influence shows itself in the fine wine lists.

Shopping

Traditional local crafts include finely woven pandanus hats, bags and mats and the intricately decorated tapa, made from paper-thin beaten bark and used as "cloth" in the pre-European era. The cool and comfortable all-purpose paréo (*pareu*) is a unisex garment much like an Asian sarong. Brilliantly colored *tifaifai* are appliquéd or patchwork cloths produced on a number of islands. Hibiscus flowers and breadfruit tree leaves are the most popular Polynesian designs, but motifs vary from island to island.

Colorful *pareu* cover-ups are available at souvenir stands throughout the islands.

Sculpture and wood carving are particularly renowned in the Marquesas. Paintings, prints and posters are produced by a number of European and Polynesian artists. Monoi is a blend of coconut oil perfumed with the fragrance of the tiare flower. It is widely available as a moisturizing cream, soap, shampoo, sunscreen and perfume, and is used in a variety of other forms. Polynesian songs featuring the guitar and ukulele, and more traditional drum-backed dance music, are found on tape and CD and make good souvenirs. Black pearls, culti-vated in the Tuamotus, are a major factor in the French Polynesian economy and are widely available both mounted and unmounted. The most permanent Polynesian souvenir is a tattoo, an art form that has enjoyed a major resurgence in recent years.

Activities & Attractions

JEAN-BERNARD CARILLET

Despite French Polynesia's sybaritic reputation, a visit to the islands is not just a case of lazing back to gaze at the lagoon with an icy *mai tai* in hand. A visit to the islands can be extremely energetic quite apart from the scuba diving opportunities.

First and foremost, there are all sorts of activities on the lagoon. It's possible to **rent boats**—either outboard runabouts or, if you want to paddle around, kayaks or pirogue (the traditional canoe with outrigger)—or book a guided **lagoon excursion**, including snorkeling stops at the best spots in the lagoon. You can explore the often deserted motu that encircle many island lagoons. **Surfing** is enjoying a renaissance in French Polynesia. The islanders claim that this was the real birthplace of the sport. Later on, they insist, it was exported to Hawaii. On Tahiti, Moorea and Huahine, you will probably see surfers at popular surfing breaks, generally at the passes into the lagoon. **Windsurfing** and **sailing** are also popular. **Parasailing** over the lagoons, helicopter and light aircraft **flight-seeing trips** are other possibilities.

There's an equally varied selection of activities on dry land. The high islands offer a wide range of **walking** and **mountain climbing** possibilities, some of the longer ones on Tahiti requiring overnight camping stops en route. **Horseback riding** is popular on a number of islands; the Marquesas are famous for their native horses. Bicycles can be rented on most islands, and the often rugged tracks into the interior of high islands are perfect for **mountain biking**. The more expensive hotels have **tennis** courts and other sporting facilities, and Tahiti has the only **golf** course in French Polynesia.

Athletic activities, including soccer, are popular in French Polynesia, but the No. 1 local sport and major spectator attraction is **pirogue racing**. The annual Hawaiki Nui race takes place in October or November from Huahine to Raiatea to Tahaa to Bora Bora. The three-day event attracts international competitors and has the whole country glued to TV sets or scanning the horizon.

Culturally, **Polynesian dancing** is undoubtedly the major artistic attraction. Island night performances take place several nights a week at big hotels on the main islands. There are a variety of small museums on the different islands, but the **Museum of Tahiti & Its Islands**, just outside Papeete, is certainly the finest in French Polynesia and one of the best museums in the whole Pacific. There has been a great deal of archaeological work in the islands, and many ancient Polynesian temples and other structures have been restored and rehabilitated, the finest examples of which can be seen on Tahiti, Huahine, Raiatea and the Marquesas.

Tahiti

The largest and most heavily populated island in French Polynesia offers a magnificently mountainous interior and a protected lagoon around most of the island. Papeete is by far the largest urban settlement in French Polynesia and has a wonderfully colorful **market** and a vibrant **waterfront**.

It's worth renting a car to spend a day driving around the island; the complete circuit is just 114km (70 miles), but there is enough to see to occupy the whole day. Traveling around the island clockwise from Papeete, you pass the **Tomb of Pomare V** shortly before reaching **Point Venus and Matavai Bay**, a favorite anchoring spot for the early European explorers and the place where Captain Cook made his historic observations of the transit of Venus in 1769. Later, the first missionaries landed here as well. The road continues past popular surfing spots and the **Arahoho Blowhole** to **Bougainville's Anchorage**, where the French navigator made his landfall in 1768.

Tahiti has a figure eight shape: the larger circle is Tahiti Nui, the smaller one is Tahiti Iti. **Taravao** is the midpoint between the two loops and a good jumping-off point to explore the wilder, less-visited attractions of Tahiti Iti. Just beyond Taravao are the **Botanical Gardens** and adjacent **Gauguin Museum**. A huge jumble of stones marks the site of **Marae Mahaiatea**, at one time the most impressive Polynesian *marae*, or temple, on the island. Farther along there is the **Museum of Seashells** and then **Marae Arahurahu**, the best preserved marae on Tahiti.

At this point the road approaches Papeete. The Museum of Tahiti & Its Islands is definitely worth visiting for a deeper understanding of Polynesian culture and the development of the islands. One of Tahiti's most popular surfing breaks is right offshore from the museum.

JEAN-BERNARD CARILLET

Papeete's sidewalk markets are brimming with fresh produce.

Surfers will find nirvana along the coasts of Tahiti, Moorea and Huahine.

Although the population of Tahiti is found almost entirely along the coastal fringe, it is worth making an excursion into the rugged and mountainous interior. You can even stay overnight at the **Relais de la Maroto**, a hotel in the center of the island. Walkers and climbers can also explore the mountains and climb 2,066m (6,776ft) **Mt. Aorai,** the most popular peak climb.

Moorea

Separated from Tahiti by a narrow strait, Moorea is a stunningly beautiful island with the magnificent **Cook's Bay** and **Opunohu Bay** cutting into an impressively mountainous interior. Moorea is actually a more popular tourist center than its sister island, Tahiti, where many visitors are simply in transit to other islands.

The tourist infrastructure is concentrated beside Cook's Bay and at Hauru Point, just to the west of Opunohu Bay. As on Tahiti, an island circuit is a fine way to explore the island, which is just 60km (37 miles) in circumference. Going around the island counterclockwise from the airport, you pass through **Maharepa**, which features the **Maison Blanche**, or "White House," a fine example of an early-20th-century "vanilla house," built during the island's vanilla-growing boom. The road edges around Cook's Bay through the village of **Paopao** and past the Pineapple Juice Factory, which is a major island enterprise.

The 899m (2,949ft) **Mt. Rotui** divides Cook's Bay from Opunohu Bay, and the road rounds the mountain and runs past **Kellum Stop**, the former home of a wealthy American who arrived in Moorea in 1925 and offered a home base for visiting archaeologists. On the other side of the bay is **Papetoai** with its famous octagonal church, the oldest European building in the South Pacific. Just beyond Papetoai is **Hauru Point** with the big Moorea Beach-comber Parkroyal Hotel, the equally sprawling Club Méditerranée and a host of smaller establishments.

Beyond the point the road passes **Marae Nuurua** on the way to the village of **Haapiti**, with its fine Catholic church and popular surfing break. Back on the east side of the island, **Afareaitu** is the island's administrative center and offers walks to two fine waterfalls. Completing the circuit, the Vaiare ferry dock is the arrival and departure point for the regular ferries from Tahiti, looming across the narrow strait.

The **Paopao** and **Opunohu Valleys**, inland from the two great bays, shelter a fine collection of ancient Polynesian temples and other structures. A road continues from these archaeological sites to a lookout with wonderful views over the bays separated by Mt. Rotui. Moorea has some fine walks into the dense forests that cloak the interior. The ascent to the **Three Coconut Trees Pass** is one of the best, or you can follow the walking trail from Vaiare to Paopao.

TONY WHEELER

Pirogue racing is the top local sport.

Huahine

Like Tahiti, Huahine is divided into larger and smaller parts, Huahine Nui and Huahine Iti. The island is quieter and more easygoing than Tahiti, Moorea or Bora Bora, and **Fare**, the main settlement, is the very image of a sleepy South Seas port. The island's major attraction is the archaeological complex of **Maeva**, scattered on a hillside at the northeast corner of the island. It is the most extensive ancient site in the Pacific.

Two deep bays divide the two halves of the island, and Huahine Iti, with its fine **beaches** and idyllic offshore **motu**, is even quieter and less hurried than the larger, northern half of the island. There's a scattering of small resorts on Huahine Iti, for those who want to really get away from it all. Huahine also has some of the best and most consistent **surf** in French Polynesia.

Raiatea & Tahaa

Larger and busier Raiatea and smaller and quieter Tahaa share a common lagoon. This is the yachting center of French Polynesia, with bustling yachting marinas and important yacht chartering enterprises. If you want to rent a **sailboat** to explore the archipelago, this is the place. **Uturoa**, the main town on Raiatea, is the largest town in French Polynesia after Papeete.

A 98km (60-mile) road encircles the island. From town the coast road runs south to **Faaroa Bay**, which is fed by the only navigable river in French Polynesia. Just beyond the bay is **Marae Taputapuatea**, the extensively restored archaeological site of French Polynesia's most important ancient temple.

Laid-back neighboring **Tahaa** has been dubbed the "secret island." About half the size of Raiatea, Tahaa has tiny hamlets, productive vanilla plantations and several pearl farms.

Bora Bora

If there is a postcard-perfect island anywhere in the Pacific, it is Bora Bora. Soaring volcanic peaks, lush green colors, a shimmering lagoon, the encircling chain of motu—it's all here. Scattered around the island and on the motu are some of the most luxurious hotels anywhere in the Pacific. But don't fret: Bora Bora also has a selection of much more reasonably priced places.

Vaitape is the main town on the island. A 32km (20-mile) road encircles the island, hugging the shoreline almost all the way around. During WWII a huge American military base was established on the island and a major airstrip was constructed on one of the motu, now used as Bora Bora's airport. The wartime action never reached French Polynesia, but rusting **coastal defense guns** from that period can still be seen at strategic points around the island.

Favorite activities on the **lagoon** range from snorkeling trips to pirogue excursions to motu picnics. There's also a variety of topside possibilities on the main island, including **four-wheel-drive excursions** into the interior and the ascent of **Mt. Pahia** (661m/2,168ft), the impressive peak soaring behind Vaitape.

Rangiroa

The second-biggest atoll in the world, Rangiroa's vast lagoon covers 1640 sq km (1,017 sq miles), encircled by a 200km (125 mile) long chain of islands and reefs rarely more than a few hundred meters wide. Almost the entire population of Rangiroa, the airport and most of the accommodations are concentrated in the 10km (6 miles) separating the small settlements of **Avatoru** and **Tiputa**. The Kia Ora Village Hotel is the most luxurious hotel in the Tuamotus, but there's also a wide selection of small, family-run guesthouses.

Scuba diving is overwhelmingly the major attraction at Rangiroa, but there are also great sites for snorkeling, swimming and picnics around its vast lagoon. An hour away from the Avatoru-Tiputa motu, the **Blue Lagoon**, a seductively attractive little lagoon within the lagoon, is the most popular Rangiroa excursion. Other attractions are **Les Sables Roses**, the "pink beach," at the southeastern corner of the lagoon, where coral residues give the motu sand a pink glow. On the south side of the lagoon, strange coral outcrops have given **L'Île aux Récifs**, "the Island of Reefs," its name. They stretch for several hundred meters, with basins and channels that make superb natural swimming pools.

Secluded atoll lagoons offer sanctuary among the Tuamotus.

The production of **black pearls** has become a lucrative Rangiroa enterprise, and there are a number of pearl farms open to visitors.

Manihi

Manihi's elliptically shaped lagoon is 28km by 8km (17 miles by 5 miles) and is encircled by an almost continuous string of motu. Manihi has many **pearl farms** and is one of French Polynesia's main centers for black pearl production. Visits can be arranged to a number of the operations.

Visit a black pearl farm.

Tairapa Pass, at the southwest end of the lagoon, is the main entry into the atoll. The Manihi Pearl Beach Resort is the only luxury resort outside of Rangiroa in the Tuamotus. Otherwise, the choice of places to stay on Manihi is very limited.

Fakarava

Fakarava is the second-largest atoll in the Tuamotus, outranked only by Rangiroa. It has minimal tourist infrastructure, although the completion of an airstrip has started to bring in more visitors. This is a place for a complete escape, with visits to **pearl farms** and untouched **motu**.

Most of the population is gathered in **Rotoava** village, at the northeast end of the lagoon near Garuae Pass, although a handful of inhabitants live in **Tetamanu** village, on the edge of the southern pass. On the eastern edge, an uninterrupted reef strip stretches for 40km (25 miles). Bird Island (**Îsle aux Oiseaux**), a crescent-shaped coral tongue covered in small shrubs, is a favorite place for nesting birds. The western side has a few scattered islets.

Nuku Hiva

Many of the visitors to the remote and mysterious Marquesas arrive on the *Aranui*, the cargo-passenger vessel that makes regular voyages from Tahiti to the Tuamotus and Marquesas. It is a rare opportunity to experience life on a South Seas cargo ship. Herman Melville's short visit to Nuku Hiva in 1842 provided the material for *Typee*, the first successful publication for the author of *Moby Dick*.

JEAN-BERNARD CARILLET

A *tiki* stands guard.

The largest island in the archipelago, Nuku Hiva is the only island in the Marquesas with scuba diving possibilities. **Taiohae**, on the south coast, is the main settlement, but there are the other charming villages of **Hatiheu, Taipivai** and the tiny, seductive **Anaho**. The island boasts some superb restored **archaeological sites**, with numerous ancient temples made up of big basaltic boulders and statues called *tiki*—looking like Easter Island's *moai*—terrific **walking** and **horseback riding** opportunities and a good selection of **beaches**. Unfortunately the dreaded *nono*, an intensely irritating little biting insect, is found on beaches throughout the Marquesas. Handicrafts are also notable everywhere in the Marquesas.

Rurutu

The only island in the Australs with regular scuba diving possibilities, Rurutu is the Polynesian basketwork capital and is also famous for its limestone **caves** and visits from **humpback whales,** which are here to reproduce and care for their young from July to October.

LIONEL POZZOLI

Snorkeling with humpback whales off Rurutu is a surreal experience.

Diving Health & Safety

JEAN-BERNARD CARILLET

General Health

French Polynesia is generally a healthy place for locals and visitors alike. Food and water are good, fresh, clean and readily available, though for safety's sake, it's best not to drink tap water except in Papeete and Bora Bora. There are few endemic diseases, and the most serious health problem that visitors are likely to experience is sunburn. Malaria does not exist in French Polynesia, but there have been occasional outbreaks of the mosquito-borne dengue fever, for which there is no prophylactic. Bring a good insect repellent to avoid mosquito and other insect bites. The most locally used spray is called Off!, and it is quite effective. Prevention is your wisest course to avoid coral cuts and scratches, mosquito bites, sunburn and heatstroke.

Pre-Trip Preparation

Your general state of health, diving skill level and specific equipment needs are the three most important factors that impact any dive trip. If you honestly assess these before you leave, you'll be well on your way to assuring a safe dive trip.

First, if you're not in shape, start exercising. Second, if you haven't dived for a while (six months is too long) and your skills are rusty, do a local dive with an experienced buddy or take a scuba review course. Finally, inspect your dive gear. Feeling good physically, diving with experience and with reliable equipment will not only increase your safety, but will also enhance your enjoyment underwater.

At least a month before your trip, inspect your dive gear. Remember, your regulator should be serviced annually, whether you've used it or not. If you use a dive computer and can replace the battery yourself, change it before the trip or buy a spare one to take along. Otherwise, send the computer to the manufacturer for a battery replacement.

If possible, find out if the dive center rents or services the type of gear you own. If not, you might want to take spare parts or even spare gear. A spare mask is always a good idea.

Purchase any additional equipment you might need, such as a dive light and tank marker light for night diving, a line reel for wreck diving, etc. Make sure you have at least a whistle attached to your BC. Better yet, add a marker tube (also known as a safety sausage or come-to-me).

35

Ciguatera Poisoning

Ciguatera is a type of food poisoning with potentially serious and long-lasting effects. It occurs when someone eats sufficient amounts of toxin-laden fish. The toxin accumulates when normally safe-to-eat fish ingest the ciguatera microorganism, commonly found living in algae and sea plants growing in coral rubble areas. The microorganism flourishes when the area is disturbed by things like storms, El Niño temperature fluctuations, coastal development and human pollution.

The microorganism secretes ciguatoxin, which is not fatal to the creature but is stored in the organs. When the smaller creature is eaten by a larger fish, the toxin invades the next host. Thus, large and older eels, great barracuda, groupers, snappers and other major players in the upper food chain are often the most toxic and common carriers. When it enters the human system, the toxin affects neurological, gastrointestinal and cardiovascular systems. Since some symptoms are similar to decompression sickness (DCS), ciguatoxin poisoning must be considered when treating bends cases.

The first symptoms generally appear two to 20 hours after eating the contaminated fish. Digestive upsets, itching, lip numbness, irregular heartbeat and sensory and neurological disorders are characteristic symptoms, and can range from mild to severe. Some are long-term and life changing depending on the individual's reaction. A few fatalities have been attributed to the toxin in the Pacific region.

Immediate medical treatment is of utmost importance. Mannitol, an intravenous solution, is highly regarded and effective when used early on.

There aren't many reported cases of ciguatera in French Polynesia, so don't be paranoid. Ciguatera-laden fish look and taste normal, and the toxin is unaffected by cooking, so the best strategy is to avoid eating them in the first place. When in an area reported to be infected with ciguatera, check with the inhabitants of the atoll. They'll know which species are diseased and the places to avoid fishing for them.

JEAN-BERNARD CARILLET

About a week before taking off, do a final check of your gear, grease o-rings, check batteries and assemble a save-a-dive kit. This kit should at minimum contain extra mask and fin straps, snorkel keeper, mouthpiece, valve cap, zip ties and o-rings. Don't forget to pack a first-aid kit and medications such as decongestants, ear drops, antihistamines and seasickness tablets.

Tips for Evaluating a Dive Operator

First impressions mean a lot. Does the business appear organized and professionally staffed? Does it prominently display a dive affiliation such as CMAS, NAUI, PADI, SSI, etc.? These are both good indications that it adheres to high standards.

When you come to dive, a well-run business will always have paperwork for you to fill out. At the least, someone should look at your certification card and ask when you last dived. If they want to see your logbook or check basic skills in the water, even better.

Rental equipment should be well rinsed. If you see sand or salt crystals, watch out, as their presence could indicate sloppy equipment care. Before starting on your dive, inspect the equipment thoroughly: Check hoses for wear, see that mouthpieces are secure and make sure they've given you a depth gauge and air pressure gauge.

After you gear up and turn on your air, listen for air leaks. Now test your BC: Push the power inflator to make sure it functions correctly and doesn't free-flow; if it fails, get another BC—don't try to inflate it manually; make sure the BC holds air. Then purge your regulator a bit and smell the air. It should be odorless. If you detect an oily or otherwise bad smell, try a different tank, then start searching for another operator.

DAN

Divers Alert Network (DAN) is an international membership association of individuals and organizations sharing a common interest in diving and safety. It includes DAN Southeast Asia and Pacific (DAN SEAP), which is an autonomous nonprofit association based in Australia. DAN SEAP members should call ☎ 61 8 8212 9242. DAN America members should call ☎ 919-684-8111 or 919-684-8DAN (-4236). The latter accepts collect calls in a dive emergency.

DAN does not directly provide medical care; however, it does provide advice on early treatment, evacuation and hyperbaric treatment of diving-related injuries. Divers should contact DAN for assistance as soon as a diving emergency is suspected. DAN membership is reasonably priced and includes DAN Travel-Assist, a membership benefit that covers medical air evacuation from anywhere in the world for any illness or injury. For a small additional fee, divers can get secondary insurance coverage for decompression illness. For membership questions in Australia call ☎ 03 9886 9166 or fax 03 9886 9155. In North America call

☎ 800-446-271 from within the U.S. or ☎ 919-684-2948 from anywhere else. DAN can also be reached at www.dan.ycg.org.

Diving & Flying

There is no problem in diving right after a flight—so long as you're not tired, exhausted or suffering from terminal jet lag of course—but flying right after a dive is definitely not advised. The usual advice is that you should complete your last dive at least 12 hours (some experts advise 24 hours, particularly after repetitive dives) *before* your flight to minimize the risk of residual nitrogen in the blood that can cause decompression sickness.

Careful attention to flight times is necessary in French Polynesia because so much of the inter-island transportation is by air and because international flights often depart in the middle of the night. If your flight home leaves at midnight, don't plan on diving on your last afternoon. Better yet, don't dive at all on your last day.

The only exception to this don't-dive-then-fly rule is the short hop between Moorea and Tahiti. The small aircraft used for this less-than-10-minute flight rarely go above 300m (100ft), an altitude that is generally accepted as safe for divers. It is not unknown for the Air Moorea pilots to fly especially low if a diver requests it!

Medical & Recompression Facilities

If you do need medical care, the facilities in French Polynesia are generally of a high standard and all physicians are highly qualified French doctors. The main hospital, the **Centre Hospitalier Territorial** (☎ 46 62 62) on Ave. Georges-Clémenceau in the Mamao district in Papeete treats the most serious injuries. It also has a modern, reliable recompression chamber that's used by professional divers who work for the Tuamotu pearl farms.

On the outer islands, the facilities may be limited, but in case of an emergency, patients are transferred by plane to the main hospital in Papeete. There is at least a small but modern dispensary on every populated island. These include:

Moorea: Afareaitu Hospital ☎ 56 23 23

Bora Bora: Centre médical de Bora Bora, in Vaitape ☎ 67 70 77

Raiatea: Uturoa Hospital ☎ 66 35 03

Rangiroa: Centre médical d'Avatoru ☎ 96 03 75

Nuku Hiva: Nuku Hiva Hospital ☎ 92 03 75

Drift-Diving Safety

French Polynesia is renowned for its exhilarating drift dives. Drifting with the current is part and parcel of the dive experience in many of the sites in the Tuamotu archipelago and in most of the Society Islands, where the configuration of atolls and islands combined with the tidal flows create ideal drift-diving conditions. As the tide rises and falls, powerful currents move through the lagoon, particularly around its openings (known as passes) to the ocean. Enormous volumes of water gush into the passes, forming bottlenecks and creating strong currents that can reach 6 knots. Without using your fins, you allow the current to carry you into the lagoon, where the effects of the current diminish. The sensation of being pushed or pulled is indescribable, and you may feel as though you are flying through the depths of the pass.

Drift dives in French Polynesia are almost always conducted during an ingoing tide. When the tide is going out, dives are made outside the reef, away from the pass and the current. During outgoing tide, conditions are riskier, since the current is heading for the open sea. Moreover, if the swell or the wind is going in the opposite direction to the current, a phenomenon called a *mascaret* is produced near the pass. The area becomes turbulent with whirlpools and full of suspended particles, which makes it difficult to see and much more dangerous.

Transport to the drift dive site is done by Zodiac. After all the divers have descended, the boat captain follows them by tracking their bubbles. At the end

of the dive, the divemaster inflates a marker buoy to signal the exact position of the group, and the captain picks up the divers.

Drift diving is exciting, but you should take extra precautionary measures. The main danger is of being swept away from your group. Resist the temptation to dive on your own (even with your buddy), and stay close to the divemaster. Another danger is of being injured when a current sweeps you toward a rocky pinnacle. Stay alert to your position near any rocks.

Though the divemaster has a marker buoy, all divers should carry their own signaling device, such as a brightly colored marker tube, in case they become separated.

French Polynesian divemasters are accustomed to these particular conditions and will give you advice if you are unsure of your ability to undertake any given dive. Some sites are best suited to more experienced divers, while others are manageable for novice divers.

MICHAEL MCKAY

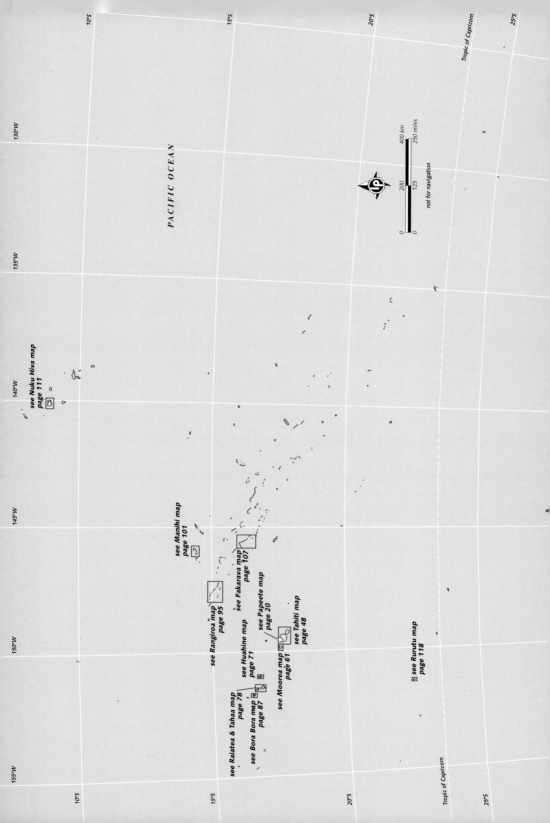

PACIFIC OCEAN

see Nuku Hiva map
page 111

see Manihi map
page 101

see Rangiroa map
page 95

see Fakarava map
page 107

see Papeete map
page 20

see Huahine map
page 71

see Tahiti map
page 48

see Moorea map
page 61

see Raiatea & Tahaa map
page 78

see Bora Bora map
page 87

see Rurutu map
page 118

400 km
250 miles

200
125

0
0

not for navigation

Tropic of Capricorn

Tropic of Capricorn

10°S
15°S
20°S
25°S

155°W
150°W
145°W
140°W
135°W
130°W

Diving in French Polynesia

PHILIPPE BACCHET

Comprising 118 islands in five widely scattered groups, French Polynesia offers a huge variety of diving opportunities.

Although most of the diving is found in two of the groups—the Society Islands and the Tuamotus—there are limited organized diving possibilities at two other islands in two other groups (Nuku Hiva in the Marquesas and Rurutu in the Australs).

The six main islands of the Society Islands Group—Tahiti, Moorea, Huahine, Raiatea, Tahaa, Bora Bora—are home to the overwhelming majority of the population of French Polynesia. These islands also include a large proportion of the region's hotel rooms and tourist facilities and, hardly surprisingly, a large part of the diving infrastructure. The main islands are all high islands, rising steeply out of the sea, and all have surrounding shallow lagoons. Good dive sites are found both inside and outside the lagoons.

To the east of the Society Islands are the scattered, low-lying islands of the Tuamotus. These classic coral atolls, which barely break the surface of the ocean, are a prime attraction for scuba divers, who are lured by the protected lagoons, dense marine life, exciting currents swirling through the passes, and steep drop-offs outside the outer reefs.

The waters of French Polynesia offer a wide variety of attractions for visiting divers, including some superb underwater topography, dense marine life, several excellent caves and even the odd shipwreck. But the big attraction is a simple one: megafauna! Divers who like to encounter the big stuff will return from French Polynesia well satisfied. On many islands it's a rare dive when you do *not* encounter sharks, whether at the somewhat contrived shark-feeding sessions at The Tiki off Moorea or the twice-daily shark "rush hour," which takes place with every incoming and outgoing tide through the passes at Rangiroa, Manihi or Fakarava.

Large marine life is also the attraction at the two sites in the Marquesas and Australs. Huge schools of dolphins and meetings with hammerhead sharks and manta rays are the main reason for diving at Nuku Hiva in the Marquesas. At Moorea a prime attraction is the friendly stingrays. Manihi and Fakarava host marbled groupers, and near Rurutu in the Australs it's the annual parade of humpback whales that attracts and awes scuba divers.

Another strong point is the proximity of the dive sites. The outer reef is never far from shore, and boat trips to get to the sites usually take just 10 to 15 minutes. Shore dives, however, are rare in French Polynesia.

41

PHILIPPE BACCHET

Though controversial, shark feeding draws many divers to French Polynesia.

Shark feeding, diving with rays, snorkeling with whales, drift diving—French Polynesia provides superb dive sites and close encounters that will seduce even the most blasé diver. Most of these dives are accessible to novice divers.

Shark feeding is a popular activity at Moorea, Raiatea and sometimes Bora Bora and Manihi. The divemaster drops down to the bottom at around 15 to 20m (50 to 65ft), signals the divers to form a semicircle and produces a large hunk of fish from a feedbag. Hundreds of fish hurl themselves on this offering, and soon blacktip, grey and even lemon sharks appear. After 15 minutes of intense activity, the remains are tossed aside and the dive continues at a calmer pace.

This practice is controversial, and not all dive centers, let alone divers, approve. Some divers have the impression of being in a contrived circus. It clearly disrupts natural behavior patterns, and it might encourage aggressive behavior in the sharks. It also leaves the fish more vulnerable to spearfishers. And, although no serious accidents have yet been reported, shark behavior remains unpredictable.

Diving with rays is less heart-poundingly intense than mingling with sharks, but just as spectacular. You may see manta rays and eagle rays at a number of sites. In the shallow waters of Moorea and Bora Bora, you will encounter stingrays so used to divers—again, feeding has helped a lot—that they will "dance" around you.

A drift dive through a pass is the major specialty of the Tuamotus. On the rising tide, as ocean water flows into the lagoon, the narrow passes create power-ful currents. Outside the pass, divers simply drop into the flow and are swept through into the calm waters of the lagoon, accompanied by swirls of fish.

Snorkeling with humpback whales when they stage their annual July to Oc-tober migration is the major attraction at Rurutu in the Australs. Once you find the whales, all you do is don your snorkeling equipment and jump in with them.

Diving with electra dolphins (sometimes called melon-headed whales) is the highlight at Nuku Hiva in the Marquesas. On the east side of the island, hundreds of these white-lipped dolphins assemble daily; a mask, snorkel and fins are all that's necessary to join in.

Snorkeling

French Polynesia has plenty of snorkeling opportunities, whether it is straight from the shore or from a boat. There is often excellent snorkeling just inside a lagoon's outer reef, and on almost every island, trips are organized to the small sandy islets known as motu that dot a lagoon's outer reef. There will usually be fine snorkeling around these motu. Some popular scuba diving sites are also suitable for snorkeling. Intrepid snorkelers can even get their share of the region's trademark shark encounters and, of course, snorkeling with humpback whales at Rurutu.

Some sensible precautions are necessary when snorkeling in French Polynesia. The tropical sun can be intense and it's easy to forget that your back is exposed to the sun. If you're going to be snorkeling for a long time, it's wise to wear a T-shirt. Even though the waters of the lagoon are sheltered from the open sea, there can be currents and swells. Ask for local advice and keep an eye open for changing conditions. Take great care around the passes, the entrances into a lagoon from the open sea. The currents during incoming and outgoing tides can be very swift, and it's easy for an unwary swimmer to get swept right out of the lagoon on an outgoing tide. In ideal conditions it's sometimes possible to walk across the reef and swim outside the lagoon, but this should only be attempted with caution. Swimming outside the reef is generally only possible with a waiting boat.

Snorkeling in the Aquarium off Tahiti, backed by Moorea's dramatic coastline.

JEAN-BERNARD CARILLET

Certification

French Polynesia will be the first diving experience for many visitors, whether it is making a one-time "resort dive," known as a *baptême* in French, or completing a certification course. Although CMAS is the principal French scuba diving qualification and is offered by the main dive operators in French Polynesia, the well-known PADI qualification is also widely available.

A PADI dive course leading to a basic Open Water certification typically takes a week and includes a series of lectures and practice sessions, instruction in a swimming pool and finally a number of sessions in the sea. If you've come to French Polynesia with an interest in learning to dive but without actually making any prior arrangements, it's worth asking around to see what other visitors think of the courses and instructors. Courses do vary, and a good instructor can make a real difference even at the most professional operation.

Live-Aboards

Three live-aboard boats run scheduled trips in French Polynesia, primarily in the Tuamotus and the Marquesas. This is an ideal way to explore these areas, since the boats go to atolls and islands that regular dive centers cannot access. On a live-aboard trip, you'll be rewarded with pristine diving conditions at sites that have seldom been dived. Some live-aboards, for instance, offer trips to Eiao island, north of the Marquesas archipelago, a wild and remote region, or to Fakarava and Kauehi atolls, considered by many to be the ultimate French Polynesian dive destination. See the Listings section for more details on the live-aboards.

In vast, shallow locations such as the Tuamotus, inflatable Zodiacs are used to transport divers.

Dive Site Icons

The symbols at the beginning of each dive site description provide a quick summary of some of the following characteristics present at each site:

 Good snorkeling or free-diving site.

 Remains or partial remains of a wreck can be seen at this site.

 Sheer wall or drop-off.

 Deep dive. Features of this dive occur in water deeper than 27m (90ft).

 Strong currents may be encountered at this site.

 Strong surge (the horizontal movement of water caused by waves) may be encountered at this site.

 Drift dive. Because of strong currents and/or difficulty in anchoring, a drift dive is recommended at this site.

 Beach/shore dive. This site can be accessed from shore.

 Poor visibility. The site often has visibility of less than 12m (40ft).

 Caves are a prominent feature of this site. Only experienced cave divers should explore inner cave areas.

 Marine preserve. Special regulations apply in this area.

Pisces Rating System for Dives & Divers

The dive sites in this book are rated according to the following diver skill-level rating system. These are not absolute ratings but apply to divers at a particular time, diving at a particular place. For instance, someone unfamiliar with prevailing conditions might be considered a novice diver at one dive area, but an intermediate diver at another, more familiar location.

Novice: A novice diver should be accompanied by an instructor, divemaster or advanced diver on all dives. A novice diver generally fits the following profile:
◆ basic scuba certification from an internationally recognized certifying agency
◆ dives infrequently (less than one trip a year)
◆ logged fewer than 25 total dives
◆ little or no experience diving in similar waters and conditions
◆ dives no deeper than 18m (60ft)

Intermediate: An intermediate diver generally fits the following profile:
◆ may have participated in some form of continuing diver education
◆ logged between 25 and 100 dives
◆ dives no deeper than 40m (130ft)
◆ has been diving in similar waters and conditions within the last six months

Advanced: An advanced diver generally fits the following profile:
◆ advanced certification
◆ has been diving for more than two years and logged over 100 dives
◆ has been diving in similar waters and conditions within the last six months

Regardless of your skill level, you should be in good physical condition and know your limitations. If you are uncertain of your own level of expertise for a particular site, ask the advice of a local dive instructor. He or she is best qualified to assess your abilities based on the site's prevailing dive conditions. Ultimately, however, you must decide if you are capable of making a particular dive, a decision that should take into account your level of training, recent experience and physical condition, as well as the conditions at the site. Remember that conditions can change at any time, even during a dive.

Tahiti Dive Sites

Tahiti may be the largest, most important and most populous island of French Polynesia—in addition to having one of the world's most romantic names—but it is not the regional scuba diving center, at least from the visitor's point of view. In fact, most of the dive operators in Tahiti cater primarily to the local expatriate population. As a result, being able to understand and speak a little French is more important here than at the more tourist-oriented dive operations on the other islands. It also helps to bring more of your own dive equipment, as the local divers generally do and the operators are less equipped to rent gear.

The diving at Tahiti is rather different from the other islands of the Society Group in that there are fewer large species. Divers familiar with the waters around Moorea, Bora Bora and other Society Islands are used to encountering sharks and rays on virtually every dive. Around Tahiti it is principally the smaller fish as well as the topography, with impressive walls, that are of greatest interest.

Tahiti dives divide neatly into two categories. Tahiti is shaped like a figure eight, with Tahiti Nui as the larger loop, Tahiti Iti as the smaller. Most Tahiti Nui sites are close to Papeete, but despite the proximity to what is now a relatively large metropolis, the dive conditions are generally quite good. Tahiti Iti dives are at the opposite end of the island from Papeete, where the population is very light.

Almost all the dives are off the western coast, protected from the prevailing easterly winds. This ensures typically calm conditions, though swell from the west and currents may occasionally exert an influence.

Visibility is usually greater than 30m (100ft) except when it has rained for several days, which washes out the island and clouds the sea with runoff.

French Polynesia's largest island, Tahiti consists of two halves connected by a narrow isthmus.

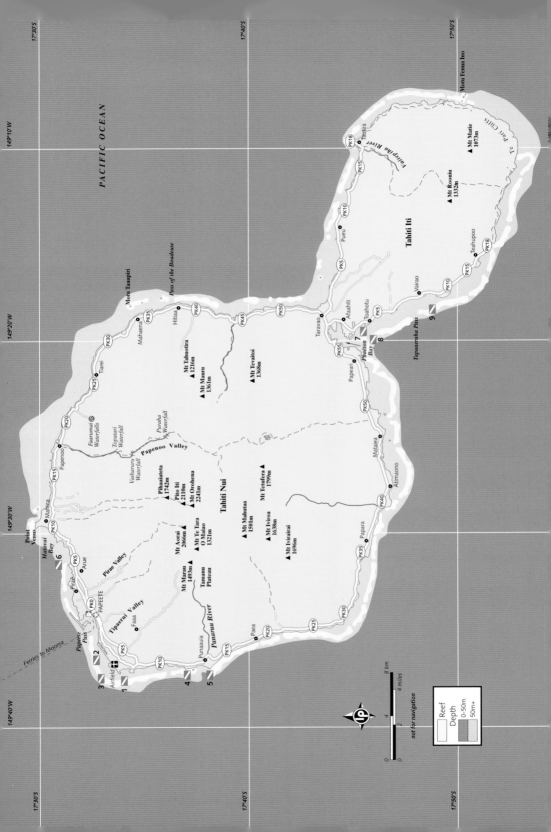

Tahiti Nui Dive Sites

	Good Snorkeling	Novice	Intermediate	Advanced
1 The Aquarium	●	●		
2 The Cargo Ship & the Catalina (La Goélette et le Catalina)			●	
3 Papa Whisky			●	
4 St. Etienne Drop-Off (Le Tombant St.-Etienne)			●	
5 The Spring (La Source)			●	
6 The Faults of Arue (Les Failles d'Arue)			●	

Tahiti Iti Dive Sites

	Good Snorkeling	Novice	Intermediate	Advanced
7 The Hole in the Lagoon (Le Trou du Lagon)			●	
8 The Tetopa Grotto (La Grotte de Tetopa)		●		
9 The Marado			●	

1 The Aquarium

Close to the end of the Faaa airport runway and near the Beachcomber over-water bungalows, The Aquarium is probably Tahiti's most popular dive site. Though it boasts nothing exceptional, its unique profile and idyllic setting are a real treat—not to mention the superb view of Moorea's jagged coastline in the background. Not surprisingly, all levels of divers as well as snorkelers and photographers make the most of it.

The terrain is basically a large sandy basin inside the lagoon with a depth ranging from 3 to 14m. It has a variety of attractions: turquoise water, coral bommies surrounded by numerous small fish and three small wrecks—a Cessna at 7m

Location: In the lagoon, off the north-west coast

Depth Range: 3-14m (10-46ft)

Access: Boat

Expertise Rating: Novice

and two small schooners between 10 and 14m. First dives are usually conducted at the lip of the basin.

This coral garden is in fact man-made, the work of Henri Pouliquen and his divemasters from Tahiti Plongée. Using large inflatable buoys, they moved hundreds of tons of coral and deposited them in the area in the mid 1980s. They used the same technique to move the Cessna and the schooners here a decade later. These artificial reefs are magnets for hosts of small colorful fish that provide macrophotographers with great opportunities in clear water. Damselfish, surgeonfish, Moorish idols, triggerfish, lionfish, angelfish and butterflyfish all flit among the bommies, and anemones play host to clownfish. The wrecks are accessible, and beginners can experience their first wreck-dive thrills sitting in the Cessna or swimming through the hull of one of the schooners. For more experienced divers, this is an ideal site to refresh their skills before taking on deeper dives. The only drawback is the occasional current.

PHILIPPE BACCHET
A diver explores the shell of the Cessna at The Aquarium.

2 The Cargo Ship & the Catalina (La Goélette et le Catalina)

About two-thirds of the way down the Faaa airport runway, inside the adjacent lagoon, this dive site features a shipwreck and an aircraft wreck. The goélette, a 30m cargo ship, lies on the sandy lagoon bottom, canted over at 45° and sloping downward. There is a mooring tied to the rudder at 10m, so finding the ship is simple. The ship's propeller is at 13m, just above the seafloor.

The superstructure has long collapsed, although the funnel still pokes up from the midsection. Inside is a jumble of wires, pipes and collapsed beams, and though it's not a penetration dive, be cautious around the tangle of wreckage. Swim the length of the ship to the

Location: In the lagoon, off the northwest coast

Depth Range: 10-25m (33-82ft)

Access: Boat

Expertise Rating: Intermediate

bow, which is resting on the bottom at about 25m, then follow the outside of the hull back to the starting point. This is an impressively large ship. The wooden hull cladding has mostly rotted away, and the wooden ribs look like a skeleton, a vivid impression heightened by the many schooling fish swimming throughout.

Continue away from the ship, in line with its axis, and in a few minutes you'll reach the other wreck, a twin-engine WWII-vintage Catalina flying boat, which was scuttled in 1964. Although the engines and almost all the interior fittings have been salvaged, the 15m structure is intact and in fine condition, its right wing tip resting on the seabed at about 20m. The other wing tip is at only 9m, and the crew's seats look out from the cockpit at around 17m. It is easy to swim in through the right-side cargo door and through the plane to emerge on the flight deck, where you can even "take the controls." The open hatch above the flight deck permits an equally simple exit.

Swim back toward the ship and up the sandy slope to make a safety stop beneath the dive boat. Small stands of coral dotting the sand provide some interest, including at least one with a healthy population of anemones and their resident clownfish.

Take the controls of the Catalina flying boat.

3 Papa Whisky

Papa Whisky takes its name from the small manmade island in line with the Faaa airport runway. There is a landing light and a radio beacon, and the call sign is "Papa Whisky." The dive site is directly in line with runway and the island, but outside the reef.

The dive boat anchors off the reef and divers drop down to a sloping shelf running from the reeftop to between 5 and 10m depth before dropping off steeply. There is plenty to see at 20 to 25m in the wide curve of the reef wall, though as at most Tahiti dive sites, you'll typically find smaller species. Bluestripe snappers follow you, clouds of small damselfish hover around the coral, and bannerfish and butterflyfish sail majestically by. If

Location: In the lagoon, west of the airport runway

Depth Range: 10-25m (33-82ft) and 40-50m (131-164ft)

Access: Boat

Expertise Rating: Intermediate

you peer into the coral you'll spot small damselfish, particularly the black and white striped humbug, and pretty little crabs. Look in crevices for the occasional boxfish.

Deeper down, starting at around 40m, are beautiful stretches of gorgonian coral.

4 St. Etienne Drop-Off (Le Tombant St.-Etienne)

Just outside the reef at Punaauia, 10km west of the center of Papeete, this site takes its name from the St. Etienne church, a prominent landmark.

Location: Off Punaauia, northwest of Tahiti

Depth Range: 10-25m (33-82ft)

Access: Boat

Expertise Rating: Intermediate

The dive boat moors immediately off the reef. Divers swim to the reef flat, which is in 3 to 5m of water, then fin to the edge of the drop-off, which tumbles away into the abyss. There is an overhanging cliff at between 30 and 50m, but there's plenty to see between 10 and 25m, and some of the best coral is found around 15m.

Divers can descend to their desired depth and then swim along the drop-off for about half the dive before turning around and returning toward the boat, gradually heading to the surface as the dive progresses.

As with any drop-off dive, it is vital to carefully monitor your depth. This is generally a small-species dive with a wide variety of coral types and the many small fish that inhabit this type of terrain. A wide assortment of triggerfish, butterflyfish, angelfish and damselfish all make an appearance, and you'll also encounter anemones with their resident clownfish. Look toward the surface occasionally, as larger species do pass by.

It is possible to enjoy a safety stop lazing around on the top of the reef before swimming back to the dive boat, but be aware that the site is exposed to the southwest swell.

PHILIPPE BACCHET

Curious morays are among the residents of this steep drop-off.

5   The Spring (La Source)

Outside the reef, directly offshore from the Museum of Tahiti & Its Islands, freshwater springs bubble up from the ocean floor. It is easy to locate the small source directly beneath the mooring spot because the fresh water looks greasy and out of focus as you swim into it and feels noticeably cooler than the surrounding seawater.

The spring is at the 20m base of a coral mount, rising up from the ocean floor. It is one of three nearby and reaches 7 or 8m from the surface, falling straight down to 25m on the seaward side and then sloping away into deeper water.

After examining the spring, you can swim around the mount, inspecting the coral and many smaller fish. The next mount, slightly to the east, is at a slightly greater depth. Its base is around 30m on the seaward side, its peak some 12m from the surface. There is a wide variety of coral and marine life, and turtles are regularly encountered. On the top there are several anemones with their resident clownfish colonies. A little farther to the east is a third mount, really a double peak with a valley in between.

Exploring the three mounts will easily fill an entire dive, but you could also head west from the first mount to another freshwater spring, closer to the reef edge. It's in only 7m of water, and the water gushes out from a vent larger than the first spring. Just beyond is a

Location: Off Punaauia, northwestern coast

Depth Range: 7-30m (23-98ft)

Access: Boat

Expertise Rating: Intermediate

little amphitheater of beautiful coral formations surrounding a small sand stage. The abundant fish life includes schools of bluestripe snappers, which are a feature of so many Polynesian dives. The dive ends at the original mount, where you can make a convenient safety stop around the top of the peak. Be cautious of the swell, which can roll in from the southwest and cause surgey conditions at times.

PHILIPPE BACCHET
Bluestripe snappers are a common Polynesian species.

6 The Faults of Arue (Les Failles d'Arue)

This is one of the few sites on the east coast, in Matavai Bay. Visibility and marine life are not the dive's strongest points, but its unusual topography makes it worthwhile. The reef here is submerged, consisting of a large plateau starting at about 6m and gently sloping to about 20m. On the ocean side, the plateau is bordered by a sheer drop-off that sinks into the abyss. The profile of the drop-off is very contoured. It's broken up by a series of crevices, fissures and overhangs, giving it a peculiarly sculpted look.

The main features are two narrow rifts that form indents in the plateau, at between 6 and 30m—hence the name "*faille*" (fault). The rifts are extremely narrow at the top, becoming wider at the bottom. Beware if you enter them from the top when there is a current—you could be sucked in and perhaps

Location: Matavai Bay, east of Papeete

Depth Range: 6-27m (20-89ft)

Access: Boat

Expertise Rating: Intermediate

bump against the coral. On the way down, don't forget to explore the undercuts, nooks and crannies that dot the sides of the rifts, where soldierfish, sweepers and lionfish tend to hide.

You can then swim along the drop-off at about 25m before gradually rising to 20m and reaching the shallowest portion of the plateau. Marine life along the drop-off is far from being abundant, but you will probably come across moray eels, surgeonfish and triggerfish. Back on the plateau, you'll enjoy good coral formations and more prolific marine life, including a vast array of small fish lurking among the coral bommies. Stay close to the edge of the wall so you don't miss the large crescent-shaped coral "window" with a big boulder in the middle that overlooks the wall, adding a nice touch to the dive.

This site is fully exposed to easterly or northeasterly winds and is best avoided in these conditions—current and swell are too rough to manage.

PHILIPPE BACCHET

Graceful gorgonians sweep down from the undercuts.

7 The Hole in the Lagoon (Le Trou du Lagon)

As the name suggests, this site features a large circular basin inside the lagoon, connected by a channel to the rest of the lagoon. An interesting dive offering a range of terrain and varied marine life, this "lagoon in the lagoon" has a smooth, sandy floor that gently slopes down to 27m. As you enter the water, numerous surgeonfish, triggerfish and remoras will keep you company. The divemaster will lead you to several coral bommies scattered along the sides of the basin.

Between 15 and 20m there is a coral boulder around which batfish usually hang. Look for a field of anemones that blanket the coral outcrops at about 10m. From time to time it pays to look toward the surface, as you may be lucky enough to spot a squadron of leopard rays. They are frequently seen in the morning, either

Location: Off Tahiti Iti's southwestern coast, in the lagoon

Depth Range: 10-27m (33-89ft)

Access: Boat

Expertise Rating: Intermediate

in the basin itself or in the channel. There's also a good chance of seeing whitetip reef sharks. After crossing the basin, swim toward the channel. The sand flats here reveal creatures not found on the reefs, especially tiny garden eels that tunnel into the seafloor. Lie without moving on the sandy bottom and you will see hundreds of them popping up like straws. This is a very unusual sight in French Polynesia. As you swim back to the boat, you will come across snappers and unicornfish.

PHILIPPE BACCHET

You may spot whitetip reef sharks resting along the sides of the basin.

French Polynesia's Sharks

PHILIPPE BACCHET

Sharks are definitely the No. 1 attraction in French Polynesia, one of the best places in the world for shark encounters. Despite their sinister reputation, they are not a concern for divers in French Polynesia. The sharks found in the lagoons, outside the reefs and around the passes are not dangerous unless provoked. Observing sharks is simply one of the enjoyments of diving in these islands. You will likely encounter at least some of the following species:

Silvertip reef shark (*Carcharhinus albimarginatus*) Strongly territorial, the silvertip reef shark is usually found on the outer slopes of the reefs. It is easily identified by the white tip on its dorsal fin and can reach up to 3m in length.

Blacktip reef shark (*Carcharhinus melanopterus*) Less than 1.8m in length, the blacktip reef shark is frequently found inside the lagoon as well as on the reef slopes.

Grey reef shark (*Carcharhinus amblyrhynchos*) Timid but also curious, the grey reef shark is not so common around the Society Islands but is regularly encountered in the Tuamotus. A uniform gray color, it reaches a maximum length of 2.5m.

Lemon shark (*Negaprion acutidens*) The lemon shark is easily identified by its slightly beige to yellow color and its two identical dorsal fins. Up to 3m in length, lemon sharks are usually larger and

PHILIPPE BACCHET

PHILIPPE BACCHET

more ponderous looking than the other reef sharks. Generally encountered farther down the reef slope, this shark tends to keep very close to the sea bottom.

Whitetip shark (*Triaenodon obesus*) This small species is primarily found resting in the sandy channels of the lagoon or the passes, as well as undercuts, facing the current.

Hammerhead shark (*Sphyrna mokarran* and *Sphyrna lewini*) These sharks are easily distinguishable by their hammer-shaped heads. In the Tuamotus, the *mokarran* species can reach up to 5m in length. Several dive sites at Nuku Hiva in the Marquesas are noted for their scalloped hammerhead shark (the *lewini* species) population.

PHILIPPE BACCHET

8 The Tetopa Grotto (La Grotte de Tetopa)

Close to the Tetopa Pass, the Tetopa Grotto features a cavity that penetrates well into the reef. The entrance is at 8m, but the grotto gradually rises up to 2m, almost reaching the reef crest. There's a main cavity with resident sweepers and various little shoals of small fish. At the back of the cavity you swim up through a tunnel into a smaller cavern. Though

Location: Tetopa Pass, off Tahiti Iti's southwestern coast

Depth Range: 3-8m (10-26ft)

Access: Boat

Expertise Rating: Novice

PHILIPPE BACCHET

Bring a dive light with you to explore the Tetopa Grotto tunnels.

you have to go one diver at a time, the tunnel is easy to negotiate and you should not feel apprehensive. Despite some small openings in the ceiling, a flashlight is needed for navigating through the tunnel.

The caverns, nooks and crannies on both sides are worth close inspection since they shelter large concentrations of lobster and soldierfish. At the back of the second cavity, hiding in a small tunnel, you'll find a group of puffer-

fish. If the site does not keep you busy for a whole dive, the divemaster will lead you to another nearby grotto—actually a big fissure in the reef, as the upper part is open. Exploring the drop-off is generally of no great interest, since the visibility is often mediocre. The site is not diveable when there is a southwestern or western swell, which would thrust divers back and forth in the grotto and make the dive very uncomfortable.

9 The Marado

This site best characterizes the type of dive you can expect to find in Tahiti Iti. It begins on the edge of a sheer wall—in fact, it's a section of the outer reef that plunges steeply to a great depth. Its main feature, apart from its spectacular profile, is the abundance of gorgonians that decorate the wall from a depth of about 20m downward—a very uncommon sight in French Polynesia. Visibility is often good and the gorgonians make a perfect backdrop, so don't forget to bring your camera. Nudibranchs can also be spotted, as well as soft corals, though the latter start at 35m.

Apart from invertebrates, the area along the wall is pretty much barren of marine life. But the exciting profile of the dive more than compensates. There are two chimneys in the wall, the first one at 25m, with an exit at 18m, allowing only

Location: Off Tahiti Iti's southwestern coast

Depth Range: 20-29m (or 35m) (66-95ft or 115ft)

Access: Boat

Expertise Rating: Intermediate

one diver at a time. The second one is at 29m, with an exit at 16m. The dive finishes on the reef crest, between 10 and 5m. This section is riddled with small canyons and coral boulders, and there is much more fish action here, including Napoleon wrasse, blacktip reef sharks, trevallies and snappers. The frequent appearance of moray eels in the open water also enlivens this dive.

PHILIPPE BACCHET

The edge of this sheer wall is draped in delicate gorgonians.

Moorea Dive Sites

A narrow strait is all that separates Moorea from Tahiti, but the flavor of the two islands—both above and below the water—is very different. The more heavily populated Tahiti is the business island, and Moorea is the tourist island. It is the same story below the waterline: Tahiti dive operators cater mainly to local residents, while Moorea's are aimed at visitors. The dive sites themselves are also quite different. At Moorea you regularly encounter sharks and other large marine life species, which are a regular feature of dive sites throughout French Polynesia, although they're strangely absent at Tahiti.

Moorea's dive operators are concentrated in the two north coast tourist enclaves at Cook's Bay and Hauru Point. As a result, most diving is focused in that area too. Inside and outside the reef and at the entrances to Cook's Bay and Opunohu Bay, the two great fingers of water lunge in toward the center of the island. The outer reef along the north shore of Moorea has colorful and varied coral that shelters a rich variety of small and large marine life. Unlike some of Tahiti's reefs, the reefs here do not drop off steeply, but slope gently away in a series of canyons, valleys and promontories.

One highlight of many Moorea dives is totally artificial and subject to some controversy: fish feeding. Fish feeding is a contentious subject among dive operators the world over. On the one hand, it undeniably alters the normal habits of marine life. On the other hand, it is undeniably spectacular and popular with many divers. One Moorea dive operator resolutely refuses to engage in fish feeding, but a bag of fish

Moorea's scuba operators cater primarily to visiting divers.

scraps is part of the dive equipment offered by most operators around Moorea. Whether or not it is wise to encourage sharks to think of divers as a reliable meal ticket is worth pondering as you watch the fish swirl around the divemaster.

Visibility is often excellent around Moorea. As for coral growth, the first 20m are rather unremarkable—there is much dead coral—but if you go deeper, you will have some great surprises.

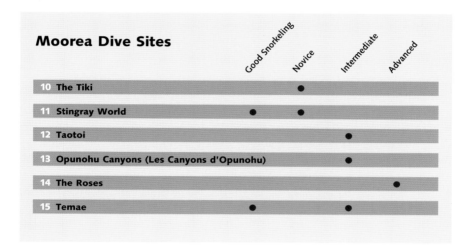

Moorea Dive Sites

	Good Snorkeling	Novice	Intermediate	Advanced
10 The Tiki		●		
11 Stingray World	●	●		
12 Taotoi			●	
13 Opunohu Canyons (Les Canyons d'Opunohu)			●	
14 The Roses				●
15 Temae	●		●	

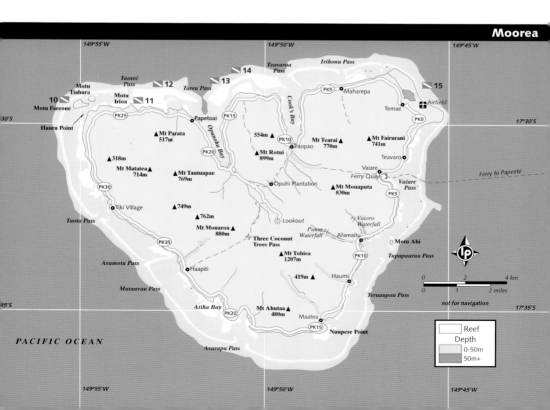

10 The Tiki

One of the most popular dives in French Polynesia is just beyond the outer reef at the northeast corner of the island. It's just to the east of Motu Fareone, which in turn is right in front of the Moorea Club Med and its prominent Tiki Restaurant. On their way out to the site, dive boats exit the lagoon via the narrow Taotoi Pass in front of the Moorea Beachcomber Parkroyal and turn east to follow the reef to the site.

The Tiki site is a long sweeping coral wall, falling away from the outer reef edge. The coral itself is not of great interest on this dive; the fish are the main attraction. There are many of them, and

Location: Northeast corner of the island, off Motu Fareone

Depth Range: 10-25m (33-82ft)

Access: Boat from Hauru Point

Expertise Rating: Novice

they are active because of the site's long history of fish feeding—and shark feeding in particular. The dive boat typically moors in 10 to 12m depth, and after assembling on the bottom, the divers swim down the reef slope to around 20m.

Blacktip reef sharks are the most commonly encountered sharks at The Tiki but you may also see grey reef sharks, and large lemon sharks are not uncommon.

The dive is subject to strong currents when big swells are running up on the reef. However, the currents can sweep away any particles in the water and reward you with exceptional visibility. At other times you can enjoy both calm water and stunning clarity, as much as 100m in ideal

PHILIPPE BACCHET
Lemon sharks are regular guests at the feedings.

Joseph Banks & Motu Irioa

Any Moorea visitor staying at Hauru Point, where many of the island's hotels and most of the dive operators are concentrated, will notice a small, low-lying, scrub-covered motu, just to the west of the two larger motu opposite Club Med. Tiny Motu Irioa enjoyed a brief but interesting moment in the history of European exploration of the Pacific. When Captain Cook was making his historic measurements of the transit of Venus from Tahiti, in 1769, he was concerned that after the long voyage from England, all it would take was one badly timed passing cloud to ruin the whole project. He therefore established two secondary measuring posts, one of them, manned by Joseph Banks, on Motu Irioa. Banks was the young scientist who played such a key role in the Cook expedition's research. Later, as Sir Joseph Banks, he was for many years the president of the august Royal Society.

conditions! It is worth noting how quickly even the most nervous divers become utterly blasé about sharks. Fifteen minutes into a dive at The Tiki and sharks—the Polynesian varieties at least—seem to utterly lose their scare power.

11   Stingray World

Lounging on the decks of their over-water bungalows, guests at the luxurious Moorea Beachcomber Parkroyal Hotel would hardly guess there is so much underwater excitement just a stone's throw away. Stingray World is only minutes from the hotel's dive center; snorkelers can easily swim out to the site. This dive is more-or-less exclusive to the hotel's resident dive center, partly because it is in what could easily be defined as the hotel's territorial waters, but also because it is Bathy's Club dive instructors who have encouraged the rays to be so friendly.

Divers usually step into meter-deep water, before their BCs and tanks are passed down to them. This depth is fine for snorkeling with the rays but it is better to swim a little farther out from the shore, to where the sandy bottom drops in a gentle slope down into the pass. Descending to about 10m gives more room for the rays to maneuver and you are less likely to stir up the sand; the rays are here because they are interested in what gets stirred up, so the visibility is expected to be less than perfect.

The prospect that you might have some tempting tidbit encourages the rays to approach you, groping with their ventral mouths for what they cannot see with their dorsal eyes. Officially, only the

Location: Off Moorea Beachcomber Parkroyal, at northwest corner of the island

Depth Range: 10-17m (33-56ft)

Access: Boat from Bathy's Club, or shore from Moorea Beachcomber Parkroyal

Expertise Rating: Novice

divemaster feeds the rays, usually with small chunks of fish. Late afternoon, after 4pm, is prime time for viewing, when as few as two or three or as many as a dozen stingrays may turn up. Some of them will have a wingspan of more than a meter. The approved technique is to kneel on the bottom and let them approach you. Gliding smoothly toward

PHILIPPE BACCHET

A stingray's skin is smooth and silky to the touch.

you, only a few centimeters above the sandy bottom, the rays simply undulate over you. They are quite unconcerned about you running your hands over them or even gently holding on to them. As they glide over the top of you, you can see their steadily opening and closing mouth and lines of gill openings. The barbed sting toward the tip of their tail; you would have to hold them down and stand on the sting to be in danger.

It is worth looking up into the blue occasionally, as far more shy eagle rays may make a more furtive appearance. You can also descend the sandy slopes another 5m to some reasonably interesting rocks and coral formations.

12 Taotoi

Taotoi Pass is just west of the large Opunohu Pass and only a couple of minutes by boat from the Beachcomber Parkroyal promontory. It is a typical Moorea dive, featuring a gradually sloping reef cut by numerous valleys, ravines and chasms.

All the usual coral and fish are encountered, but the dive has a couple of king-size regulars, at least one of which has been named by divers. One of these

Location: Taotoi Pass, off the north-eastern corner of the island

Depth Range: 10-23m (33-75ft)

Access: Hauru Point

Expertise Rating: Intermediate

residents is Jojo, a big, friendly Napoleon wrasse who rushes to greet visiting divers. You might also see a very large

Jojo the Jumbo

One of the most famous longtime residents of Taotoi Pass is Jojo, a Napoleon or humphead wrasse. Napoleons often grow to an impressive size, but Jojo truly tips the scales. He (she?) is more than a meter long, with a build like a sumo wrestler. And he doesn't keep his appetite a secret.

Jojo has learned that a visit from divers can mean free food. In fact, Jojo lumbers right in and demands to be fed. If divers form a circle, Jojo simply barges into the middle, pushing between divers or slipping beneath a raised arm like a long-lost friend looking for a hug. He'll settle for a snack.

PHILIPPE BACCHET

resident moray eel, so unconcerned about divers that it will actually emerge completely from its retreat. Usually morays just stick their heads out, but this one is halfway out of the cave before you even appear.

13 Opunohu Canyons (Les Canyons d'Opunohu)

Off the outer reef, just east of the northeast corner of Opunohu Pass, are the canyons that have become a major center for that popular Moorean activity, shark feeding. This is one of the most visited dive sites in French Polynesia and a surprising number of new divers make this their first post-qualification open water experience. Though the abundant coral and wide variety of marine life are appealing, fish feeds are the major draw, which attract fish in large numbers, sharks in particular.

The site consists of a series of canyons radiating out from the outer reef. It is regularly dived without the added excitement of shark feeding; blacktip reef sharks are usually encountered along this reef, and feeding is not necessary to ensure their presence. You may see a wide variety of other fish, including some very large triggerfish. Moray eels frequent some spots on the reef and turtles are often encountered. Clownfish and groups of damselfish hang around the anemones. Look for lionfish hiding away in small caverns

Location: Opunohu Pass, off Papetoai village

Depth Range: 10-22m (33-72ft)

Access: Boat

Expertise Rating: Intermediate

and crevices and for parrotfish grazing on the coral.

The dive site is subject to swell when large waves break on the reef. The swell can create strong surge in the canyons, making the dive difficult and rather murky, though not so strong that it cannot be dived. A pod of dolphins may accompany the boat back into the lagoon—the perfect end to any dive.

Butterflyfish gather among the anemones carpeting the reef.

PHILIPPE BACCHET

Shark Feeding in Moorea

The Tiki and the Opunohu Canyon dive sites, with their abundant coral and wide variety of marine life, are fine dives in their own right, but attracting fish in large numbers, and sharks in particular, by offering free feeds has become the major attraction. Whether or not this is a good idea is open to debate.

When your divemaster slings his tank on his back and then slips a shiny steel mesh glove on his hand, it's clear you are going fish feeding, and equally clear you are not offering tidbits to the little guys. Heading down to the bottom with a large sack over his shoulder, the divemaster looks like a submarine Santa, and evidently there are a lot of good kids at the bottom of the chimney. The sack contains a large hunk of fish carcass, and almost instantly the divemaster is surrounded by a shimmering cloud of smaller fish. Like a scuba Pied Piper, he kicks lazily away with Moorish idols, butterflyfish, surgeonfish, snappers and groupers crowding in from all sides.

Following the divemaster to the feeding spot is like being in the center lane of a freeway with faster cars overtaking you on both sides. The cars being sharks, of course. Check your rearview mirror for a glimpse at the traffic jam behind you—blacktips, greys and a host of smaller fish.

At the selected feeding spot, the divers drop down to the bottom, circle around the shark feeder and wait for the performance to begin. He is soon in the middle of a maelstrom of fish. Bluestriped snappers swirl around him, larger emperors and rainbow jacks move in from the outside, an occasional triggerfish sidles in slowly to see if there's something to grab and the sharks patrol purposefully back and forth on the outer edge of the whirlwind, waiting to pounce when their moment comes.

Soon it's time for the *repas des requins*, mealtime for sharks. The steel-gloved divemaster dips into his sack and pulls out a hunk of fish. Up to this time the smaller fish have been squabbling for the scraps that fall out of the bag. Now, with a more substantial snack on offer, it is suddenly evident that the attendant sharks' regular patrolling is just a steady high-speed cruise. When it is time to put the pedal to the metal, a shark simply explodes forward. In fact, there is only one word to describe their power—awesome. A blacktip reef shark, then another and another, rush to the scene and tear off hunks of the fish, ripping it away with a shake of the head and then launching away from the small fish frenzy. Then, as if on cue, they melt away and a much larger and more ponderous-looking lemon shark lumbers onto the stage. For several minutes at a time it may be hard to work out what's happening in the swirl of tails and fins, as one shark after another materializes, ripping and tearing at the offerings.

PHILIPPE BACCHET

At times the feeder, crouched on the bottom, pushes up several meters higher and is immediately followed by the whole gang in what looks like a volcanic eruption of fish. The diver is in the center and around him is the feeding swirl, spreading out as it drops toward his starting point. Finally, the remains are stuffed back into the sack and the larger fish peel away instantly. The dive continues across the reef with the dutiful procession of smaller fish once again fanning out behind the divemaster.

14 The Roses

The Roses ranks among the most spectacular sites in the Society Islands. However, it is a deep dive suitable only for experienced divers. Approximately halfway between Opunohu Bay and Cook's Bay, off the outer reef, The Roses features a huge field of *Montipora* coral that stretches as far as the eye can see.

Location: North of the island, between Opunohu Bay and Cook's Bay

Depth Range: 30-40m (98-131ft)

Access: Boat

Expertise Rating: Advanced

The dive starts with an impressive descent into the blue to 30m, where divers start to inflate their BCs. Looking down, you will see looming, enormous *Montipora* coral formations that blanket the bottom and that could easily be taken for petrified lettuce. Their convoluted and flattened shape is their adaptation to the scarce light penetrating these depths. It allows them to capture the maximum amount of light, necessary for their growth.

Depending on your abilities and on your divemaster's judgment, you might descend to 40m to hover over this field for a closer look at the coral. It is vital to monitor your depth and time since you are in the blue. Divers normally finish their dives by heading back toward the reef, where they explore the canyons while making their decompression stop. Depending on sea conditions, the boat is either at anchor or picks up the group at the end of the dive near the reef, for an easy drift dive.

The eerie atmosphere is what makes this dive so exciting. Don't expect swarms of fish. If you are lucky, you will see a couple of lemon sharks and blacktip reef sharks cruise by, as there are feeding sites close by. The scenery is very photogenic, and visibility is often excellent. Photographers should get great pictures of these gorgeous coral formations.

PHILIPPE BACCHET

"Blooms" of *Montipora* coral give the site its name.

Putting the Focus on Sharks!

Photographing sharks may well be one of the greatest challenges found in open ocean underwater photography. Unlike other large predator wildlife photography, in which one hides behind a 400 to 600mm telephoto lens at a relatively safe distance, in shark photography your main objective is to get as up close and personal with your subject as possible.

Focus on two distinct concerns: safety considerations and technical excellence. In terms of safety, be knowledgeable about your subjects. Listen to your divemasters: They know the sharks and their behavior. In terms of attitude, all sharks are different. There are well over 300 species of sharks, of which only a handful could be considered man-eaters or, more precisely, man-biters. Dealing with a mako, a tiger, an oceanic whitetip, a great hammerhead, a great white or other aggressive blue-water shark entails a very different approach than photographing reef sharks such as silvertips, blacktips, whitetips or greys. Fortunately for divers in Tahiti, most (though not all) of the sharks are reef sharks.

Never forget that any shark can become unpredictable. Be aware of signs of aggressive behavior such as the lowering of the pectoral fins, arching of the back or a side-to-side motion of the head. If this occurs, be prepared to retreat for a moment. Dark wetsuits and black gloves are always recommended on shark feeds. Bright colors are attractive, and pale hands can be mistaken for food.

Use the shortest focal length lens with which you are comfortable. A Nikonos with a 20mm or 15mm lens is highly recommended for fast-action situations. In more stable and predictable situations, a housed system with a 20mm lens for full-frame shots or a 24mm lens for close-ups is excellent, as are zoom lenses in the 20 to 35mm range. If you have the nerve to get within 2 to 3 feet of your subject, a full-frame fisheye lens (14 to 16mm depending on the manufacturer) is an excellent tool, capturing multiple sharks and divers in a single frame. Your tool of choice must ultimately be dictated by your photographic vision. Can't make up your mind? Take a couple of systems.

Supplemental lighting by underwater strobes is essential but presents special considerations. Sharks, like many marine predators, are bicolored (dark on top and light on the bottom) thus allowing them to fade into the background. It is very easy to overexpose the belly, so consider this in your strobe-to-subject distance and strobe power. A single strobe can be used successfully, but two strobes are better. Power down the strobe aimed at the belly—it should be used to soften and feather hard shadows. Your primary strobe should illuminate the subject's face and back, as well as the mask of any diver in the frame. To minimize backscatter, use oblique angles and avoid lighting the water between you and the subject. The sharks will most definitely muddy the water.

PHILIPPE BACCHET

Above all, relax and enjoy the moment. You are in the presence of some of the most imposing and memorable creatures on the face of the earth.

—*Michael Lawrence*

15 Temae

Only at the northeast corner of Moorea is there no lagoon between the coast and the reef. Here the drop-off from the fringing reef is only a stone's throw from the shore. The dive can only be made when the seas are gentle, and it is usually only dived from Cook's Bay, since it is inconveniently far from the Hauru Point dive operations.

The reef drops gently from sea level to 15 to 20m, where a sandy slope continues into the deep blue. Coral ridges reach like fingers down into the sand, and fingers of sand probe up into the coral. The dive boat anchors in 10m of water. You start the dive by swimming out to the sand, where conger eels wave in the current like some strange white vegetation. If you approach, they disappear back into their holes.

The sand's monotone uniformity can easily lead you to greater depths than you planned. Instead, swim straight out, as if you are planning to fin to Tahiti at 20m depth. It is a curious sensation to be at such a deep mid-level with the surface and the bottom equally visible. Most marine life stops where the reef

Location: Off the northeast corner of the island

Depth Range: 10-22m (33-72ft)

Access: Boat from Cook's Bay

Expertise Rating: Intermediate

turns to sand, but barracuda often pass by in the open water. During certain seasons giant triggerfish lay their eggs in the sand and are fiercely protective of their territory. They will approach you head on, snapping with their small but powerful jaws.

Back on the reef there are hosts of butterflyfish, a variety of triggerfish, quite a few anemones with their attendant clownfish, parrotfish grazing the coral and shrimp hiding in small crevices or between the branches of coral. Moorish idols bank gaudily by, and lizardfish perch on the edge of rocks, waiting for something foolish to come within their reach, while the occasional bigger grouper or wrasse swims past.

Approach slowly to watch swaying conger eels slip down into their burrows.

Huahine Dive Sites

About 170km (105 miles) northwest of Tahiti, Huahine is the first of the Leeward Islands. It's actually two islands: Huahine Nui (Big Huahine) and Huahine Iti (Small Huahine). It is green, lush and beautiful, just like other Society Islands, but it also boasts a more laid-back atmosphere that entices visitors to relax.

The island features excellent diving suitable for every level of diver. Novice divers in particular will feel comfortable. The outer reef gently slopes down, visibility is good and currents in the passes are easily manageable. And inside the lagoon, there is excellent snorkeling. In a nutshell, the dive conditions are less challenging than anywhere else but still offer excellent fish action, including numerous sharks. The two main dive areas are the northeastern and southern tips of the island.

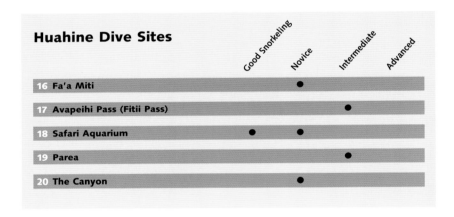

Huahine Dive Sites	Good Snorkeling	Novice	Intermediate	Advanced
16 Fa'a Miti		●		
17 Avapeihi Pass (Fitii Pass)			●	
18 Safari Aquarium	●	●		
19 Parea			●	
20 The Canyon		●		

Crystal-clear Huahine lagoon offers protected diving and excellent snorkeling.

PACIFIC OCEAN

16°42'S

151°02'W · 151°00'W · 150°58'W

16°42'S
16°44'S
16°46'S
16°48'S
16°50'S

16

Airfield

Lake
Fauna Nui

Motu
Oavarei

Maeva · Ancient Stone
Fish Traps

▲ Mt Tapu
429m

Avamoa
Pass

Vaiparao

Fare

Haamene
Bay

Tevaipoopoo

▲ 271m

Motu
Mahara

20 · Tiare Pass

17
Avapeihi Pass
(Fitii Pass)

▲ Mt Turi
669m

Vaiumete

Faie Bay

Motu
Vavaratea

Cook's
Bay · Fitii

▲ Mt Puuaretu
220m

Huahine Nui

Faie

▲ Mt Paeo
440m

Lookout

▲ Mt Tavahi
347m

Vaioaa

Faterea Pass

Motu Topati

▲ 261m

Maroe Bay

▲ Le Doigt
180m

Motu
Murimahora

Mt Veihi ▲
198m

Mt Faaua ▲
186m

Bourayne
Bay

Maroe

Huahine Iti

Motu
Vaiorea

Tefarerii

▲ 409m

▲ Mt Puhueri
462m

Tiapaa
Bay

Haapu

Mahuti

Mahuti
Bay

▲ 322m

Parea

Avea
Bay

Motu
Araara

18

19

Araara Pass

N

0 ___ 1 ___ 2 km
0 ___ .5 ___ 1 mile

not for navigation

Reef
Depth
0-50m
50m+

16 | Fa'a Miti

Fa'a Miti lies at the northwestern tip of Huahine, just before the airstrip and in front of the Huahine Village Hotel. The immersion point is close to the shore, since the reef practically fringes the coast and there is no lagoon. Though less popular than Avapeihi Pass, Fa'a Miti has many assets and is only 10 minutes by boat from Fare. Conditions are optimal at all times—there is neither current nor big swell, the setting and layout are pleasant and the visibility is often excellent. Unlike at Avapeihi Pass, do not expect many grey reef sharks in the vicinity. Reef life, moray eels and coral formations are what this site is all about.

The outer reef follows a moderate sloping profile. At about 20m, the reef is broken by a small sandy valley where local divemasters often hand-feed the fish, which immediately congregate around the divers. Regular feeding has made many of these fish exceedingly approachable, which is ideal if you want to

Location: Northwestern tip of the island

Depth Range: 10-25m (33-82ft)

Access: Boat

Expertise Rating: Novice

shoot up close. Look for stingrays that might be buried in the sand. At around 25m, the dive area is dotted with small, well-preserved clusters of *Porite* and elkhorn coral, amid which you will see saddletail perch, large triggerfish, snappers, trevallies, unicornfish, surgeonfish, damselfish and several species of butterflyfish.

Heading back toward the anchor, take the time to carefully explore the overhangs where soldierfish swarm and crevices and fissures form recesses for moray eels. Some of the eels are semi-tame and easily approachable. If you are lucky, you might see them leaving their shelter and swimming in open water.

PHILIPPE BACCHET

Although sharks aren't plentiful at Fa'a Miti, other marine life abounds in its recesses and open water.

17 Avapeihi Pass (Fitii Pass)

This dive site, only five minutes by boat from Fare village on the west coast of the island, is renowned for its concentrations of barracuda, Forster's seapikes, trevallies and grey reef sharks. Unlike other sites in the Leeward Islands, there is no regular shark feeding in the area. Predators are naturally attracted to the vicinity of the pass, which is plentiful with reef fish.

The pass is approximately 300m wide and is sheltered from the prevailing winds, thus offering good dive conditions at all times. The best opportunity to spot predators is during an outgoing current, when they patrol the pass in search of drifting lagoon fish. The only drawback is the slightly reduced visibility, which averages about 20m.

The usual immersion point is on the north side of the outer reef. Swim along the reef toward the beginning of the pass. At 15m the reef forms a plateau that gently slopes down to the sandy bottom of the channel, at 30m. Most fish congregate above this strategic point and along the northern side of the pass, sparing the effort to cross it. You will come upon schools of barracuda, humpback and bluestriped snappers, tuna, surgeonfish, parrotfish, Napoleon wrasse, triggerfish, butterflyfish, trevallies and as many as 20 to 30 grey reef sharks, providing an excellent opportunity for wide-angle photography.

Depending on the strength of the current, you might have to hold on to the bottom to swim in the pass. In that case, keep an eye toward the surface, otherwise you might miss the schools of eagle rays hovering over you.

Location: Off Fare, on the western coast

Depth Range: 15-25m (49-82ft)

Access: Boat

Expertise Rating: Intermediate

Coral is not the strong point of this dive, apart from some yellow *Stylaster* carpeting a small wall at 20 to 25m where the outer reef meets the pass.

PHILIPPE BACCHET

Strong currents support a wealth of marine life.

18 Safari Aquarium

The highlight of this dive is its idyllic setting. Located inside the lagoon, close to the barrier reef and southwest of the island, it offers fantastic snorkeling conditions. Imagine a huge swimming pool with pristine turquoise water dotted with a multitude of coral heads around which a profusion of small reef fish congregate. Add the Huahine Iti Mountains and

Location: Off the southwestern tip of the island, in the lagoon

Depth Range: 2-3m (7-10ft)

Access: Boat

Expertise Rating: Novice

This vast shallow expanse is a snorkeler's paradise.

JEAN-BERNARD CARILLET

Motu Araara as a backdrop, and you have a great snorkeling spot. The site it is too shallow for diving.

Boat access is needed, since the reef is too distant from the shore. The coral pinnacles here are numerous in an otherwise sandy lagoon. In fact, this vast field of brightly colored coral heads festooned with anemones and partially mantled by encrusting sponges belongs to the barrier reef. The quality of the coral is excellent, and if you want to shoot macro, this site is for you. Clams and urchins are numerous, and the usual array of reef fish adds life and color. Pufferfish, damselfish, triggerfish, bluespotted groupers and bagnards play amid the coral formations. Do not neglect the seafloor. It harbors many large stingrays resting or rooting through the sand patches while searching for crustaceans and worms.

19 Parea

On the southwestern side of Huahine and directly off of Parea village, this site offers an excellent opportunity to dive in a largely unspoiled area with good coral development and excellent visibility. Unlike other drift dives in Polynesia, this dive doesn't take place in the pass itself but on its outer sides. Parea Pass presents no interest for it is too shallow, the current and surge are too strong to be negotiated and the visibility is poor. All things considered, conditions for this dive must be calm for it to be dived safely.

Location: Off the southwestern coast of the island, close to Parea Pass

Depth Range: 25-40m (82-131ft)

Access: Boat

Expertise Rating: Intermediate

You enter the water about 20m from the reef, and there is no specific itinerary. Divers swim off and along the barrier reef at a depth between 25 and 40m and drift with the current. Colonies of boulder coral—mostly 2 to 3m high—dot the bottom and provide refuge to a variety of marine life. Look for snappers, parrotfish, Moorish idols and moray eels that shelter in the nooks and crannies.

Coral formations come in various species: elkhorn, fire coral and *Porite*. The topography is gentle, and the reef mildly slopes down to 40m and beyond. Local guides don't feed the fish, and sharks are less frequent than at other sites, but the current brings its fair share of pelagics, including trevallies and shoals of barracuda, and turtles may also be spotted in the vicinity.

The boat picks divers up at the end of the dive. Visibility is excellent, and if you master the current, you can get excellent wide-angle and close-up photographs.

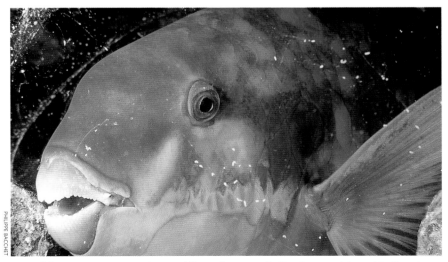

PHILIPPE BACCHET

Parrotfish secrete a mucous sack around themselves as protection from predators while they sleep.

20 The Canyon

Don't expect a huge concentration of fish life during this dive—at least in the first section. The topography is the main attraction. Located in Tiare Pass, east of the island, The Canyon well deserves its name. It consists of a large corridor flanked by steep cliffs decorated with soft and hard coral.

The bottom of the pass is at 27m but it isn't necessary to go that deep. Divers usually follow the drop-off to the left or right, according to the choice of the dive instructor, and explore fissures and cavelets sheltering moray eels. You will come across yellow *Stylaster* coral and some sponges that could be a potential subject for your camera.

Location: Tiare Pass, east of the island

Depth Range: 12-20m (39-66ft)

Access: Boat

Expertise Rating: Novice

The topography then starts to differ substantially as the canyon progressively widens out and the cliff-like drop-off gives way to a flat coral garden where fish life is much more prolific. The usual species of reef life play amid coral pinnacles at about 12 to 15m, and you will have plenty of photo opportunities.

Steep canyon walls in Tiare Pass give way to a flat coral garden flush with schooling fish.

PHILIPPE BACCHET

Raiatea & Tahaa Dive Sites

Between Huahine and Bora Bora, the twin islands of Raiatea and Tahaa share a common lagoon. A narrow 3km (1.9-mile) channel separates the two islands. Less touristed than their neighbors, the islands offer an opportunity to enjoy a more old-fashioned and relaxed Polynesian lifestyle.

Raiatea is the largest of the Leeward Islands and is outranked in the whole Society Group only by Tahiti. It is vaguely triangular in shape with an encircling road that hugs the coast all the way around. The interior is mountainous and includes the 800m-high Temehani Plateau. Uturoa, the principal town on Raiatea, is the largest town in French Polynesia after Papeete, and it's the administrative center for the Leeward Islands. Often referred to as "Sacred Raiatea," the island played a central role in ancient Polynesian religious beliefs.

Tahaa is a quiet little place with a 70km road winding around most of the convoluted coast. Apu Bay to the south, Haamene Bay to the east and Hurepiti Bay to the west are deep, superb inlets that are favorites for visiting yachties. Tahaa has few tourist facilities, and traffic is very light. Visitors who want to get away from it all will find Tahaa a perfect haven.

The diving in both islands is excellent and varied. One of the rare wreck dives in French Polynesia is available in Raiatea—the *Nordby*—featuring a 50m vessel

PHILIPPE BACCHET

One of French Polynesia's few wreck dives, the *Nordby* lies directly beside a luxury resort.

just offshore. Apart from truly remarkable marine life—including sharks, of course—Tahaa and Raitea also boast an interesting seascape, with seamounts and numerous caverns and small grottoes along the sides of the reef.

Another attraction is the abundance of beautifully colored yellow and purple *Distichopora* coral that adorns the caverns and drop-offs.

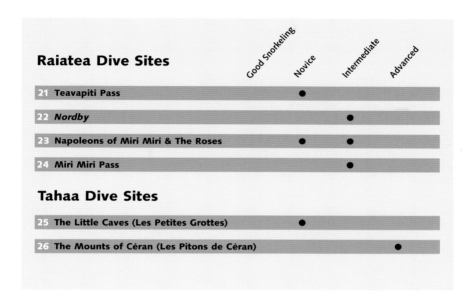

Raiatea Dive Sites

	Good Snorkeling	Novice	Intermediate	Advanced
21 **Teavapiti Pass**		●		
22 *Nordby*				●
23 **Napoleons of Miri Miri & The Roses**			●	●
24 *Miri Miri Pass*				●

Tahaa Dive Sites

	Good Snorkeling	Novice	Intermediate	Advanced
25 **The Little Caves (Les Petites Grottes)**		●		
26 **The Mounts of Céran (Les Pitons de Céran)**				●

21 Teavapiti Pass

Off the eastern coast of Raiatea, Teavapiti Pass is a must. It is a multilevel site where divers are guaranteed to see masses of fish, both reef species and pelagics. Best dived during an incoming tide or at the end of an outgoing tide, it features a coral ridge outside the pass at 17m that runs perpendicular to the pass.

A typical dive plan consists of swimming along both sides of this ridge, watching the schools of fish and predators, and then drifting with the current along one of the sides of the pass. Your best bet for fish action is to swim along the side exposed to the current, where most predators congregate to hunt.

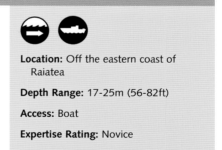

Location: Off the eastern coast of Raiatea

Depth Range: 17-25m (56-82ft)

Access: Boat

Expertise Rating: Novice

The quantity and variety of fish will amaze you. Sharks—whitetips, greys and blacktips—as well as several species of big trevallies, barracuda, Napoleon wrasse, eagle rays, surgeonfish, triggerfish, batfish, butterflyfish and Moorish idols, to name a few, are a common sight. When the tide is going out, visibility is often reduced, but this is compensated by the rewarding sight of even denser concentrations of pelagics, including tuna. You finish your dive close to one of the sides of the pass, where the boat picks you up. Do not ascend in the middle of the channel, since Teavapiti Pass is the main access into the lagoon for cruise ships and schooners.

Teavapiti Pass features a wide variety of fish, both pelagics and reef dwellers such as soldierfish.

22 *Nordby*

The *Nordby* is the best wreck dive in French Polynesia—a relatively easy distinction due to the scarcity of wrecks in Polynesian waters. She lies on her side on a sandy bottom, literally at the foot of the over-water bungalows of the Hawaiki Nui Pearl Beach Resort, between 18 and 29m, and is accessible from the pontoon of the hotel.

She measures 50m in length, which means that in a single dive you can explore the inside and outside of the ship at leisure. The ship is relatively well preserved, with few fissures in the iron hull. You enter her through a hole near the rudder and can explore the hold at about 20m. It is very atmospheric and quite safe to explore. The whole of the ship is acces-

Location: Off the eastern coast of Raiatea

Depth Range: 18-29m (59-95ft)

Access: Shore

Expertise Rating: Intermediate

sible, and light filters through the side from the girders of the bridge. A flashlight is strongly recommended if you want to see the resident fish that hide in the darker parts, including groupers, soldierfish, angelfish, Moorish idols, lionfish, a couple of moray eels and various species of crustaceans.

PHILLIPE BACCHET

Parrotfish are among dozens of residents amid the wreckage.

The three-masted *Nordby* plied the Papeete-Liverpool route, carrying copra and wood. The vessel sank in August 1900 after a storm drove it ashore. You will see the anchor, the chain and the two main masts protruding from the bridge on the seaward side, as well as the winches used to handle the yards. Soft and hard species of coral colonize the in-terior, including black coral and *Dendro-phylia* that blankets the ceiling. The coral outside is poorer, but small nudibranchs crawl along the hull.

Visibility in this part of the lagoon is often reduced due to runoff from a nearby river.

The *Nordby* is also a superb night dive, when many shellfish emerge to feed.

23 Napoleons of Miri Miri & The Roses

This site must be a divemaster's dream. It has everything and suits all levels of divers, in clear and calm waters. On the northwestern side of Raiatea, just off the barrier reef, it is protected from swell, winds and current, thus guaranteeing spectacular visibility. Photographers will be delighted by the perfect conditions that prevail and will make the most of their wide-angle setup.

Location: Off the northwestern coast of Raiatea

Depth Range: 15-20m or 40m (49-66ft or 131ft)

Access: Boat

Expertise Rating: Novice/Intermediate

PHILIPPE BACCHET

Experienced divers will appreciate the patches of *Montipora* coral thriving at 35 to 40m.

There is a tremendous amount to see along the gently sloping reef at a depth of less than 20m. As soon as you enter the water, you'll be surrounded by hordes of small fish looking for food. Photographers will find them very cooperative. But the major attraction is a couple of enormous semi-tame Napoleon wrasse. They have become used to divers and you'll have an opportunity to interact with them. Swimming closer to the reef, you will see schools of Forster's seapikes, snappers, parrotfish and trevallies. Sharks, both whitetips and blacktips, also patrol the area. At the end of the dive, while exploring the *hoa*—the small channels carved into the upper reef crest—you may spot schools of fish in less than 4m. Schools of needlefish regularly swim near the surface.

The only weak point of the dive is the poor condition of the coral. But ad-vanced divers can venture about 15m deeper to admire the breathtaking field of *Montipora* that flourishes at a site called **Les Roses**.

To visit Les Roses, the typical dive plan is sl ghtly modified. Divers get dropped off in the deep, a bit farther out. Blacktip reef sharks soon make their appearance. Descend to 35 to 40m where vast expanses of *Montipora* in pristine condition will take your breath away, forming a striking contrast with the first barren 20m. Anchored on the reef, it flares out like huge rose petals to capture the maximum amount of light. You then come up to 30m, over a ridge separated from the sloping reef by sand channels that provide an ideal resting place for whitetip reef sharks. Schools of snappers are also a common sight. The rest of the dive follows the same pattern as the Napoleons of Miri Miri.

24 Miri Miri Pass

On the west coast, this interesting and varied site is sheltered from the prevailing winds and swell and offers ideal conditions. The typical dive plan is a drift dive, usually when the tide flows out of the lagoon. Visibility is reduced, but you are rewarded with much more fish action. The dive does not take place in the middle of the pass, which is devoid of interest, but on the northern side, along the drop-off. You start the dive by exploring three massive boulders about 15m from the drop-off, at approximately 30m, around which numerous fish whirl.

Before swimming toward the drop-off, look into the caverns at the base of the boulders where whitetip sharks tend to rest. Its main interest is not the hard coral, but the superb and photogenic *Distichopora* species whose bunches carpet the wall from about 20m to the bottom. Bring a flashlight to get the full impact of its lovely purple hue. Black coral is also prolific here.

Location: Off the western coast of Raiatea

Depth Range: 22-30m (72-98ft)

Access: Boat

Expertise Rating: Intermediate

Proceeding farther, you come to a scenic arch carved into the wall at 28m, bringing some variety to a reef that would otherwise look uniform. After the arch, the scenery changes again with a flat section at about 20m, which boasts prolific fish life, including schools of trevallies, surgeonfish, barracuda, Napoleon wrasse, Moorish idols, groupers, triggerfish and angelfish by the dozen. Apart from the whitetip sharks at the beginning of the dive, don't expect to see any other sharks during this dive. For shark action, the Teavapiti Pass dive site is superior.

PHILIPPE BACCHET

Delicate bunches of purple *Distichopora* coral adorn the wall from about 20m to the bottom.

25 The Little Caves (Les Petites Grottes)

Though close to Les Pitons de Céran, this site is totally different. Here the fish action is not the dive's strong point. What makes it distinctive is the topography, as well as the abundance of *Distochopora* coral that adorns the caverns carved into the sides of Toahotu Pass.

Location: Toahotu Pass, east of Tahaa

Depth Range: 15-25m (49-82ft)

Access: Boat

Expertise Rating: Novice

Most dives take place along Motu Toahotu, at the southern side. You will drop to about 20m and explore the undercuts and caverns, where bunches of delicate, yellow *Distichopora* flourish. Most fish congregate in the middle of the pass and around the Pitons, so don't expect many encounters. A couple of Napoleon wrasse and the usual reef species are the most probable sights.

Cup corals prefer shaded areas such as this site's many undercuts and caverns.

PHILIPPE BACCHET

26 The Mounts of Céran (Les Pitons de Céran)

In Toahotu Pass, between two idyllic motu east of Tahaa, this is undoubtedly the island's most attractive site. Get your wide-angle lens ready, as the visibility is superb at incoming tide and fish are numerous. The boat usually anchors on the reef top, at 10m, close to one of the motu. You descend to about 32m and swim over the pass floor, which looks like a valley, until you reach a small ridge at 28m. During this first part of the dive, don't forget to keep looking up toward the surface, as there is a good chance of spotting eagle rays, schools of barracuda and batfish hovering in the open water.

Location: Off the east coast of Tahaa

Depth Range: 25-39m (82-128ft)

Access: Boat

Expertise Rating: Advanced

When you reach the ridge, two seamounts come into sight in the background. They are actually two large pinnacles rising just off the ridge. This striking topography exudes an eerie atmosphere, making this site unique. You then swim around the bigger seamount and stop at a little overhang that forms a perfect observatory at 35m, overlooking the seafloor some 15m below. The place is sheltered from the current, and you can lie comfortably on the coral to watch fish action.

You're sure to see a few whitetip reef sharks, angelfish, marbled groupers, Napoleon wrasse and soldierfish in the cav-

erns, and schools of trevallies and surgeonfish spinning around the seamount in compact orbit. When you have seen all there is to see, let yourself be carried into the lagoon, where the boat picks you up.

Apart from the yellow *Stylaster* coral that peppers the caverns in the ridge, don't expect rich coral formations. Fish action and scenery are what this site is all about, and they more than compensate for the lackluster condition of the coral.

PHILIPPE BACCHET

Look for the spectacular emperor angelfish around the seamounts.

Bora Bora Dive Sites

JEAN-BERNARD CARILLET

The topside scenery is world famous.

Bora Bora is 270km (167 miles) northwest of Tahiti and only 15km (9 miles) northwest of Tahaa. The main island stretches about 9km in length and about 4km in width. A 32km (20-mile) road runs along the coast. A wide, sheltered and navigable lagoon encircles the island, with sandy motu edging most of the outer reef. Matira Point, at the southern tip, is bordered by a magnificent beach. It's also where most of the tourist infrastructure is concentrated.

This seductive island has dive sites inside and outside the lagoon, and all of them enjoy the unbeatable bonus of having the island—with its soaring mountains, turquoise lagoon and green and gold motu—as a backdrop as you travel to and from the sites.

Manta rays and sharks are the trademark large marine life encountered inside and outside the lagoon. Bora Bora also has fine coral and a wide variety of smaller fish and sea creatures. If there is a catch to diving at Bora Bora, it's that there is only one pass into the lagoon. Some of the dive sites involve a long boat trip across the lagoon, through the pass and around the outside of the reef to the site.

Bora Bora Dive Sites	Good Snorkeling	Novice	Intermediate	Advanced
27 Anau	●	●		
28 Toopua & Toopua Iti	●		●	
29 Tapu			●	
30 Muri Muri/The White Valley (La Vallée Blanche)			●	
31 Tupitipiti			●	

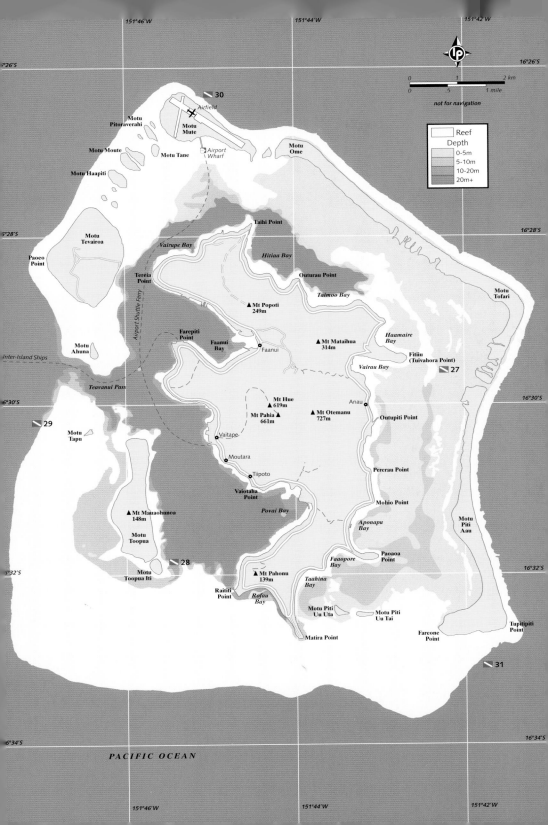

27 | Anau

Manta rays are the major attraction of this dive inside the lagoon off Fitiiu (also known as Tuivahora) Point, on the east side of the island. The mantas use the sandy pass, which bottoms out between 20 and 25m, to travel north and south and also to patrol the coral ridges to the east and west.

Dive boats usually anchor at the popular snorkeling spot on the east side of the pass. Divers enter the water in 5m depth and drop down over the edge of the coral-fringed reef. When you see the mantas, approach them smoothly and slowly; thrashing around and rapid movement will scare them away. You should not attempt to touch them. If you're patient, they may approach very closely. If you're lucky, you may see as many as five to 10 mantas, typically with 2 to 3m wingspans, although a huge 4m specimen may fly by.

Blacktip reef sharks also patrol the reef, often accompanied by tiny, bright yellow pilotfish scuttling along just in

Location: East of the island, in the lagoon

Depth Range: 10-22m (33-72ft)

Access: Boat

Expertise Rating: Novice

front of the shark's nose, behaving for all the world like dolphins in front of a boat.

It is also worth looking down. Moray eels, including a very bold one that has clearly become used to being fed, dwell within the reef. Clouds of threadfin butterflyfish, blackspot snappers with their distinctive yellow fins and the odd remora follow the divemaster if he or she is carrying a feedbag. Big Napoleon wrasse, a variety of other butterflyfish, longfin bannerfish, colorful angelfish, parrotfish and numerous smaller fish are regular encountered.

The high season for this dive is May to December, when the visibility is better and there are more manta rays about— you are almost 100% certain of seeing them. The mantas also give birth during this time. The visibility is generally not so good January to April, although you can get lucky and have excellent clarity. During this time your chances of seeing mantas are perhaps 40% to 50%. At times, the sandy bottom of the pass gets stirred up, making the water quite murky.

PHILIPPE BACCHET
Manta rays commonly glide through this sandy channel.

28 | Toopua & Toopua Iti

These two dives are usually done individually but may also be linked as a drift dive. Motu Toopua is the large motu running south from Teavanui Pass. Just off the southern tip of Motu Toopua is the much smaller Motu Toopua Iti. A sandy channel runs around the smaller motu, connecting the two dive sites, Toopua Iti to the west and Toopua to the east.

Eagle rays are often encountered along this channel, moving between Tekou Bay on the west side of Motu Toopua and the deep Povai Bay, which is between the motu and the main island of Bora Bora. Strong currents sometimes flow through this channel, making a drift dive possible, although this can also make for murky and less than ideal dive conditions. If you spot eagle rays, approach them very slowly and smoothly, hurried or jerky motion will only scare them away. Occasionally you'll see manta rays in this channel.

Starting from the Toopua Iti side, divers enter the water over the reef in as little as 5m depth. If the currents are cooperating, divers can head for the pass to look for the rays and follow the reef wall around to the shallower mooring spot at Toopua, a popular snorkeling site, or drop into deeper water, reaching 30m as the pass enters Povai Bay.

Alternatively, divers can follow a route directly over the reef, winding in and out of canyons, gullies, corridors, small caves and swim-throughs. The reef is

Location: Southwest of the island

Depth Range: Toopua, 5-30m (16-98ft); Toopua Iti, 5-15m (16-49ft)

Access: Boat

Expertise Rating: Intermediate

studded with giant clams, whose brightly decorated mantles offer a vivid splash of color. There are a number of anemones along this route, complete with their protected populations of clownfish. Large moray eels sometimes emerge from their hideaways to inspect passing divers. Sharks, as well as the lagoon's assortment of smaller marine life, are also seen around the reef.

PHILIPPE BACCHET

The area's varied topography includes several swim-throughs.

Snorkeling at Bora Bora

Bora Bora is not strictly the preserve of scuba divers. There are also some excellent snorkeling spots, including just inside the outer reef edge around the southern end of the island, although you need a boat to get out to it. There are popular shallow-reef snorkeling areas inside the lagoon close to the Anau and Toopua scuba diving sites. Boats sometimes take scuba divers and snorkelers to these sites.

In Front of the Bora Bora Hotel The waters directly in front of the Bora Bora Hotel, from Raititi Point toward Matira Point, offer some wonderful snorkeling. The hotel landing at the point is particularly good because hotel staff regularly feed the fish and actively discourage fishing, creating an unofficial marine reserve. Although the hotel may be unwelcoming to people walking along "their beach," beaches in French Polynesia are open to anyone, and the hotel cannot make any claim on the beach or the water in front of its guest rooms.

Motu Piti uu Uta The new Sofitel Motu Hotel is on the north side of this small motu, immediately east of Matira Point, but the prime snorkeling spot is off the southwest side of the motu. The depth reaches only 3 to 4m, and there's lots of coral and fish life. The water is so shallow that you can often walk across to the motu from Matira Point.

The Aquarium The Aquarium is a popular snorkeling site between Motu Piti Aau and the inner edge of the outer reef near Tupitipiti Point, immediately offshore from Club Med and just south of the motu beach where the resort regularly transports its guests. The site is well protected by the nearby outer reef and also enjoys a steady flow of water from waves breaking across the reef. These create perfect conditions for coral growth. As a result, the site has fine coral and a rich variety of marine life. The water is only 1 to 3m in depth, but even the odd larger fish as well as a huge diversity of smaller ones may be found. The only minor danger at the site is that if there is a big swell breaking across the outer reef, it can create strong currents inside the reef.

29 Tapu

Tapu is the original Tahitian form of taboo. No, it's not forbidden to make this dive, and no, you won't be offending any deeply held Polynesian beliefs. The dive takes its name from Motu Tapu, the small islet just south of Teavanui Pass. Once upon a time, the island was a cemetery for important burials, and visiting was most definitely taboo.

The dive is outside the outer barrier reef and, as at so many French Polynesian sites, sharks are a major attraction. The dive's dense shark population is probably a result of regular fish feeding, although

Location: West of the island

Depth Range: 10-30m (33-98ft)

Access: Boat

Expertise Rating: Intermediate

it seems to have been balanced by a decline in the number of moray eels, which were once very common.

The dive mooring is at about 15m on the gently sloping, coral-studded reef face. Even from the surface, divers may spot a blacktip reef shark or two patrolling relentlessly. The dive starts by dropping to the bottom and then descending the reef slope. If the divemaster has a feedbag, the accompanying cloud of fish might include cheeky and colorful yellow, white and black threadfin butterflyfish, often followed closely by handsome triggerfish. They are soon joined by surgeonfish and the occasional unicornfish. Hulking silvery trevallies dash in and out, while the odd Napoleon wrasse and grouper make an appearance.

Meanwhile, the blacktip reef sharks are ceaselessly moving back and forth. They are remarkably fearless and, since the current-swept water can be exceptionally clear, the shark viewing can be especially good! They may swim straight toward you, veering away at the last moment. The reef's resident lemon sharks are usually found farther down the reef. Shy creatures, although reputedly fearsome if threatened, they stick very close to the bottom, slithering sinuously among the coral heads with a grace that belies their size. The reef starts to become more open below 25m and fades into a sandy slope from around 35m.

Divers usually turn around by 30m and work their way back up the slope to around 10m, beyond their original starting point. It's worth making a closer inspection of the reef. There are gullies and canyons, the odd

overhang and all sorts of activity among the rocks and coral. An inspection of holes and openings in the reef may turn up anything from a moray eel to a couple of lionfish. After your divemaster dumps the remains of the feedbag and sharks scatter smaller fish to polish the feed off in a ravenous fashion, you'll finish the dive by heading straight back to the mooring line.

PHILIPPE BACCHET

As you hover over the reef, keep an eye out for sharks.

30 Muri Muri/The White Valley (La Vallée Blanche)

Location: North of the island

Depth Range: 15-30m (49-98ft)

Access: Boat

Expertise Rating: Intermediate

This interesting dive goes by a variety of names, including Shark Point (from its inhabitants) or The White Valley (from one of its notable features). Until you actually arrive at the northern apex of the ring of motu encircling Bora Bora, it is always uncertain if you can dive, because the waves may be too rough. Even when the water is calm, the currents that run past the point can sometimes be dangerously fast. Such currents often attract sharks, but because of regular feeding, sharks start congregating as soon as they hear a boat engine. There will usually be a respectable crowd when you enter the water.

A quick descent is recommended because of the current and the sharks. Although French Polynesia's sharks are extremely unlikely to cause any problems, it is still better to get down to their level rather than splash around on the surface, where they may take an interest in you. At around 15m, the sharks, and a wide variety of other fish, are busily picking over whatever has been tossed in for them. Grey reef sharks and black-tip reef sharks are the varieties normally encountered, and they will often swim toward you with interest, veering away as they get closer. Look for the remora or suckerfish that often accompany them.

Once you've had your fill of sharks, you can swim across the undulating terrain with bommies and outcrops of coral-studded rocks. From around 20m the coral becomes much more continuous and colorful, but at around 28 to 30m the reef edge is encountered and the drop-off steepens as it goes down to much greater depths. The White Valley

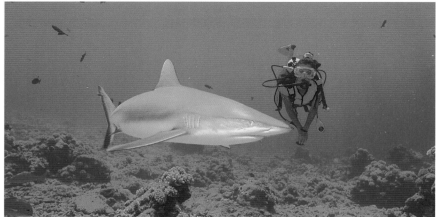

PHILIPPE BACCHET

Strong currents and regular feedings ensure visits from this site's many cruising sharks.

is a curving sandbar running for about 300m through this rock and coral terrain.

In addition to the local shark population, a large turtle and a wide variety of smaller fish are often seen around the reef. Bright blue parrotfish grate away at the coral, and yellow snappers, surgeonfish, triggerfish and soldierfish are often encountered. Silvery slender needlefish weave delicately past, bluestriped snappers come by in larger groups and a variety of colorful butterflyfish and tiny damselfish dart around the coral heads.

Look up as well as down. The visibility is usually excellent and the anchor line can be seen running right up to your dive boat. Passing by overhead you can see sharks and perhaps shoals of barracuda or jacks. Dolphins are also sometimes encountered. The dive usually finishes back under the boat where divers make their way up the anchor line to the surface.

31   Tupitipiti

Few divers experience one of Bora Bora's most magical dives. Even though it's only a stone's throw from the popular Aquarium snorkeling site at the southern end of Motu Piti Aau, it's outside the reef, a 20km, 45-minute trip even in a fast dive boat, over an hour in a slower one. Furthermore, wave and swell action can make it undiveable, and even slight swell requires great care in the caves and swim-throughs, where the effects can be dangerously magnified. Strong currents sometimes sweep around the point, but these can be used to make it a drift dive.

There is a final problem: Anchoring is very difficult because of the steep drop-off. Most regular Bora Bora dive sites have moorings, but this has not proved practicable at Tupitipiti. The usual practice is to have someone stay on the boat while the divers are below.

Only a short swim from the reef the depth drops to 50m, so divers descend to 10 to 20m in open water and then swim north to the reef edge. And what a reef edge to meet, the steep drop-off is tumbled with rocks, cut by ridges and dotted with caves, swim-throughs and overhangs. Above, you can see the waves beating against the reef edge. But down

Location: Southwest of the island

Depth Range: 10-30m (33-98ft)

Access: Boat

Expertise Rating: Intermediate

below it can be quite calm. The usual variety of smaller fish are encountered, whitetip reef sharks patrol the reef or rest in the caves and turtles sometimes swim around the point.

Marine life is not, however, the main attraction. Tupitipiti offers wonderful opportunities to enjoy the "architecture" of the coral reef, to squeeze through caves and tunnels and drift under overhangs or through chasms and corridors. Photographers will find numerous subjects. There is wonderfully delicate and colorful blue and red branching coral. Red, green and orange sponges add to the extravagant display. If you descend farther down the reef edge, yellow gorgonian coral starts at around 35m.

Rangiroa Dive Sites

Rangiroa (from Rairoa, literally meaning "long sky"), 350km (220 miles) northeast of Tahiti, in the Tuamotu archipelago, is the second-biggest atoll in the world, outranked only by the Kwajalein atoll in Micronesia. "Rangi," as it is usually called, measures 75km (50 miles) from east to west and 25km (15 miles) from north to south. From the edge of the lagoon, it is impossible to see the opposite shore. In fact, "lagoon" is an understatement to describe the immense marine spread encircled in this reef crown. "Internal sea" is more appropriate.

In two decades, Rangiroa has established itself as the most famous tourist destination in the Tuamotus. Travelers visiting French Polynesia for the first time should include it in their trip for an atoll experience. For divers from all over the world, it is a Shangri-la. It is the epitome of Tuamotu diving, with amazing drift dives. What makes diving here exceptional are the pass currents and the density of pelagics, particularly sharks. Visibility also defies description, often exceeding 40m. Everything is regulated by the tide and the current. As the tide rises and falls, powerful currents move through the openings—the passes—of the atoll to or from the ocean. In an incoming current, all you do is immerse yourself in the ocean and let yourself be propelled through the pass into the lagoon, where the effects of the current dissipate. When the tide is going out, dives are never made in the pass itself; conditions are too risky, as the current is heading for the open sea. Instead, groups dive outside the reef, along it and away from the current.

Because the distance covered during the drift dive is huge, the Zodiac follows divers' progression by tracking their bubbles. At the end of the dive, the instructor

Pacific double-saddle butterflyfish have plenty of room to roam in Rangiroa's vast lagoon.

inflates a signal marker and the boat picks up the divers. In Rangiroa, don't expect rich coral formations—the hurricanes have devastated vast fields of coral, and deposits swept along by the currents deter coral development.

Such conditions mean this type of diving is best suited to experienced divers, though there are also good alternatives for novices in the lagoon.

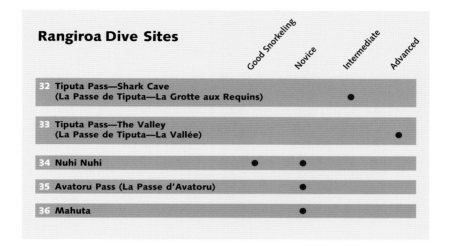

Rangiroa Dive Sites

	Good Snorkeling	Novice	Intermediate	Advanced
32 Tiputa Pass—Shark Cave (La Passe de Tiputa—La Grotte aux Requins)			●	
33 Tiputa Pass—The Valley (La Passe de Tiputa—La Vallée)				●
34 Nuhi Nuhi	●	●		
35 Avatoru Pass (La Passe d'Avatoru)		●		
36 Mahuta		●		

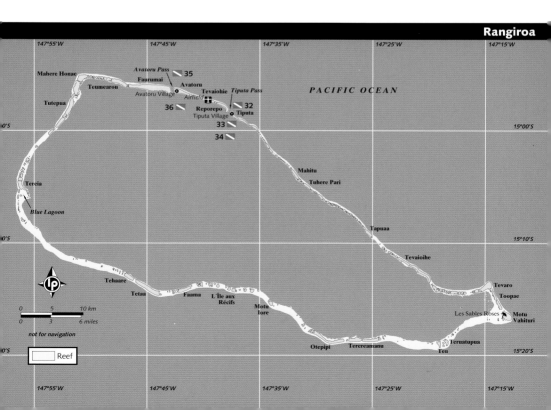

32 Tiputa Pass—Shark Cave (La Passe de Tiputa—La Grotte aux Requins)

This dive site is probably the most famous site in French Polynesia. Divers from all over the world come to Rangiroa to experience it. What makes it so unique is the shark action and the powerful current that sweeps divers through the pass. Thrilling rides are guaranteed every time. Compared to its western sister, Avatoru, Tiputa Pass boasts a stronger current and greater numbers of pelagics that are more easily observed. The scenery is wilder as well. Don't forget your camera—you'll have fantastic opportunities to approach big pelagics at arm's length.

The Zodiac will generally drop you at the edge of the reef wall, on the left exit of the pass. You'll descend quickly through intense blue water to a cave at 35m. It's actually an overhanging rock that looks like a balcony, where divers can shelter from the current and watch the show. And what a show: Grey reef sharks in bewildering numbers coast by in the

Location: North of the atoll, next to Tiputa village

Depth: 35m (115ft)

Access: Boat

Expertise Rating: Intermediate

background, from the surface to the seafloor at 45m. On certain days, the pass is so packed with these sharks that it defies description. There have been claims of sightings of up to a hundred, but several dozen sounds more realistic. There are also schools of snappers, trevallies, surgeonfish, unicornfish and groupers, as well as soldierfish hiding in the cave. From July to October, there is a good chance of seeing manta rays and eagle rays. Divers then join the pass entrance farther to the south and continue into Tiputa Pass.

PHILIPPE BACCHET

Hordes of grey reef sharks line up for mealtime outside Tiputa Pass.

33 Tiputa Pass—The Valley (La Passe de Tiputa—La Vallée)

This site is the embodiment of Tuamotu diving. If you have never experienced a drift dive, you will find The Valley unforgettable. Topographically, the pass looks like a valley—hence the name. The submarine plateau, which is very wide at the ocean mouth of the channel, narrows at the east and west rims on either side, and rises toward the lagoon to the south. Don't expect a profusion of coral. The strong current makes the formation of coral impossible, and the pass bed looks like an eroded, sterile slab.

Two dive plans are possible, depending on your experience level: You can either go to the **Grotte aux Requins** and continue into the pass or, for advanced divers only, dive straight to the bottom of the pass, about 45m at the entrance. Such a deep dive is justified by the presence of hammerheads that cruise in the depths and are generally seen between November and February. Let yourself be sucked into the pass. For about 10 minutes, you'll feel as though you're gliding, accompanied by a procession of fish, both reef species and pelagics. The depth reduces progressively, rising to 20m at the inside entrance of the lagoon.

The sensation is unforgettable. Don't stay right in the middle of the pass but try to have a look at the undercuts on the sides, replete with fish. You'll finally reach the coral boulders close to Motu Nuhi Nuhi for a convenient

Location: North of the atoll, next to Tiputa village

Depth Range: 20-45m (66-148ft)

Access: Boat

Expertise Rating: Advanced

decompression stop, where the boat picks you up.

When the tidal flow is going out, you dive along the outer reef, east of the pass and away from the current, at a site called **L'Eolienne**. Small reef life is the main feature of the site, with dolphins sometimes enhancing the show.

PHILIPPE BACCHET

Longfin bannerfish ride the current through the pass.

34 Nuhi Nuhi

Also known as The Aquarium, this site is only a few minutes' boat ride from the local dive operators. Its main draw is its strategic intermediate location. Nuhi Nuhi is a motu (coral islet) that stretches north-south across Tiputa Pass just inside the lagoon.

Though inside the lagoon, it's also in line with Tiputa Pass and is, therefore, exposed to the ingoing current at high tide that carries a fair selection of pelagics, namely whitetip sharks, manta rays and occasionally barracuda. It's better to swim in calmer water, close to the western side, which is sheltered by the northeast-

Location: North of the atoll, close to Tiputa pass, in the lagoon

Depth Range: 3-10m (10-33ft)

Access: Boat

Expertise Rating: Novice

ern tip of the islet. That's the area usually chosen by dive and snorkel operators.

In less than 10m, Nuhi Nuhi teems with all the common reef fish. Most of the local species of butterflyfish, triggerfish, snappers, damselfish, parrotfish, Napoleon wrasse, moray eels, angelfish, groupers, surgeonfish and black-striped surgeonfish can be found here. The area is riddled with alleys and a jumble of coral pinnacles that provide a haven for all kinds of vertebrates and invertebrates. Watch for giant clams, bristle worms and urchins. The coral is relatively well preserved, though hurricanes have taken their toll in some areas.

Due to Nuhi Nuhi's easy access, safe conditions and the dazzling variety of shapes and colors, it's a good site for introductory dives and training courses and for glass-bottom and snorkel boats. It's also an ideal site for divers who want to refresh their skills before taking on the more technical drift dives in the passes. As for photographers, they will make the most of the setting and of the abundance of fish that wait to have their portraits taken. The visibility is excellent at ingoing tide and photographers can concentrate on portraits and wide-angle shots.

JEAN-BERNARD CARILLET

Snorkelers enjoy calm water and myriad fish at Nuhi Nuhi.

Fish Farms

Easily recognizable by their posts, which pierce the surface of the water in channels or lagoons, fish farms are a familiar part of the landscape on many of the Tuamotu atolls.

These enclosures enable fishers to regulate the numbers of fish taken according to the needs of the inhabitants, the arrival of the schooners or the availability of air freight.

The establishment of a fish farm takes into account the currents, where the fish usually pass by and the layout of the sea bed. Generally, they are set up near channels or inside the reef ring in 2 to 4m of water. Two collecting branches, arranged in a V-shape (*rauroa*) and open at varying angles, lead to a rounded chamber (*aua*). The aua is in turn connected by a narrower entrance to a secondary hoopnet (*tipua*), placed at the side. The fish that enter this maze are unable to turn back. The fishers simply have to harpoon them or catch them in a hoopnet.

The passages, made of wire netting fixed to metal or *kahaia*-wood posts, require constant maintenance. Piled-up blocks of coral were once used for the same purpose.

JEAN-BERNARD CARILLET

35　Avatoru Pass (La Passe d'Avatoru)

Along the reef rim, on the eastern side of Avatoru Pass, this site doesn't offer much in terms of coral formations and fish life. Its main draw is the four or five massive silvertip reef sharks that haunt the area. It's not their usual habitat, but by using bait, the local divemasters have managed to settle them more or less permanently in the vicinity for the sake of amazed divers. These large predators are far more impressive than the grey reef sharks.

Divemasters normally bring a bag of dead fish that they put under coral

Location: North of the atoll, next to Avatoru village

Depth Range: 15-20m (49-66ft)

Access: Boat

Expertise Rating: Novice

branches at about 20m in a gently sloping part of the reef. You won't have to wait for long before the sharks rise up from the depths. Divers can gently hold onto a dead piece of coral boulder for leverage and watch the show. The sharks circle the bag, and their sometimes jerky maneuvers reveal a certain nervousness. Bring your camera, as it is a fantastic opportunity to get close-ups of these animals, and the visibility is often excellent.

Afterward, divers head toward the pass and, if it's slack tide or an incoming current, drift along the pass. From July to November, Avatoru Pass is a great spot to see manta rays, typically with 3m wingspans, and shoals of trevallies. The boat picks up divers in the lagoon.

36 Mahuta

Mahuta is the area that extends below Avatoru Pass, south of the small Motu Fara. It consists of an intermediary zone where clear ocean water blends with the more turbid water of the lagoon. This explains why both lagoon species and pelagics in large numbers are encountered here. It's not surprising that local fishers have set up fish "farms" nearby. The fish population is impressive and includes trevallies, barracuda, groupers, sharks—greys, whitetips and blacktips— and a vast array of smaller species.

Manta rays fly by but are less common. Apart from the density of fish, the highlights of the dive are the terrain and

Location: North of the atoll, close to Avatoru Pass, in the lagoon

Depth Range: 15-20m (49-66ft)

Access: Boat

Expertise Rating: Novice

atmosphere. At between 15 and 20m, the seafloor is carved by small parallel-running sand valleys, bounded by coral formations in good condition. These canyons look like wide cross-country ski tracks bustling with activity. While gently drifting with the fading current, explore the coral boulders teeming with fish life. Gliding over the sand canyons is an exhilarating sensation.

Ill-informed divers are often obsessed by Tiputa Pass or Avatoru Pass and tend to neglect this site. However, it's an attractive alternative to drift dives in the pass and is full of surprises. It is also a good site for novice or rusty divers who want to refresh their skills before taking on the more thrilling drift dives.

PHILIPPE BACCHET
The wide array of fish includes schooling convict surgeonfish.

Manihi Dive Sites

Some 175km (110 miles) northeast of Rangiroa, Manihi has acquired an international reputation in the field of pearl production. The first pearl farm was set up in Manihi in 1968, and the atoll has steadily established itself as a major center for black pearls in the South Pacific. The lagoon is now scattered with large-scale family and industrial pearl production farms.

This medium-size atoll has only one pass, Tairapa Pass, in the southwest, around which are the dive sites. The diving follows the same pattern as in Rangiroa

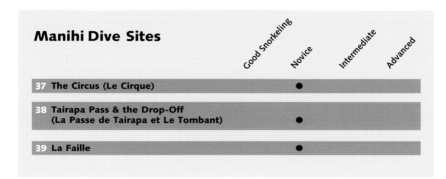

Manihi Dive Sites	Good Snorkeling	Novice	Intermediate	Advanced
37 The Circus (Le Cirque)		●		
38 Tairapa Pass & the Drop-Off (La Passe de Tairapa et Le Tombant)		●		
39 La Faille		●		

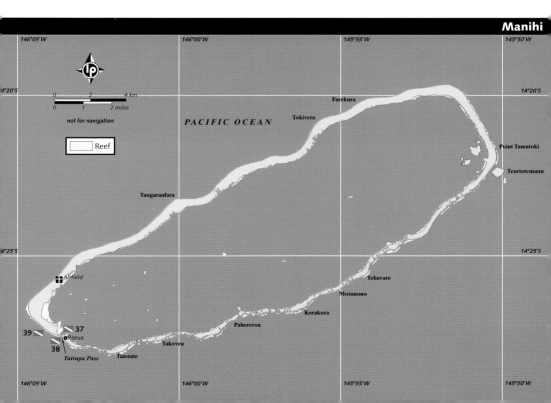

and Fakarava. The pass constantly channels nutrients in and out with the tides, attracting all forms of sea life up and down the food chain. Most dives are drift dives in an incoming current through the pass, but the outer reef also features some superb sites not to be missed.

37 The Circus (Le Cirque)

This site encompasses an area in the lagoon just beyond the shallow coral plateau at the exit of the pass. Given its location, you would expect it to be very clear at incoming tide. In reality, the plateau prevents the clear ocean water from cleaning the area properly, and the visibility is therefore limited. These conditions may seem off-putting, but the site is well worth diving due to the likeli-

Location: Southwest of the atoll, in the lagoon

Depth Range: 15-25m (49-82ft)

Access: Boat

Expertise Rating: Novice

hood of seeing manta rays and eagle rays that come to these plankton-rich waters to feed.

PHILIPPE BACCHET

Plankton-rich waters draw feeding mantas at the Circus.

While not guaranteed, superb manta experiences are possible. Photographers should have their camera ready to capture these gentle giants. Manta rays are not shy and seem more than willing to stick around for photos if you move slowly.

Another highlight is the scenic topography. Large boulders of every shape are scattered in the area between 15 and 25m and form a lunar landscape, full of atmosphere. Unfortunately, much of the coral is dead, partly due to the lack of light and oxygenated ocean water. Other fish often seen here include unicornfish, triggerfish, moray eels and sometimes schools of Moorish idols. The Circus is usually dived when the tidal current flows out. The plateau acts as a shield and prevents divers from being propelled into the pass and out to the ocean.

38 Tairapa Pass & the Drop-Off (La Passe de Tairapa et Le Tombant)

Tairapa is the only pass in Manihi. Its safe layout makes it an ideal site for both novice and experienced divers. The pass is about 100m in width, and the pass bed gradually rises from 25m at the ocean side to a shallow coral shelf at 5m before sloping gently down again into the lagoon.

Location: Southwest of the atoll

Depth Range: 5-25m (16-82ft)

Access: Boat

Expertise Rating: Novice

Three dive plans are possible, depending on the direction of the tide. When it's going out, you can dive the northern wall of the pass at a place named **Le Tombant**, away from the current. In general, you swim along the drop-off between 5 and 25m. Visibility is excellent and marine life is abundant. In July this area is a breeding site for marbled groupers, which hang around the undercuts of the reef in dense congregations.

Another option is to cross the pass from Le Tombant to the southern side. After leaving the drop-off, you literally swim under the turbid flux gushing from the lagoon, holding onto the seabed at approximately 25m. Keep an eye on the surface so you won't miss seeing the schools of barracuda facing the current, waiting for prey.

When the tide is incoming, you start your dive with a brief exploration of Le Tombant before letting yourself be carried away by the current into the pass. An incredible variety and density of fish will immediately surround you. Swim along the northen side of the pass, replete with undercuts housing soldierfish, groupers and whitetip sharks. Unfortunately, the middle and southern side of the pass are littered with tins and other objects

discarded by people living in Turipaoa, the nearby village. Finish your dive in the lagoon, and, air permitting, the divemaster might lead you to the adjacent site called **The Circus** (Dive Site #37) for an overview.

PHILIPPE BACCHET

The pass is a breeding ground for marbled groupers.

Black Pearl, Jewel of the Tuamotus

The black pearl, or *poe rava*, is a pillar of the Polynesian economy. The main centers of production are in the Tuamotu group and the Gambier Archipelago; Manihi, Fakarava, Arutua, Takapoto and Mangareva are the best known. Their lagoons, studded with pearl farms, look like lakeside towns.

The center of this activity is an oyster called *Pinctada margaritifera*, found in abundance in Polynesian lagoons. The formation of a pearl is the result of natural phenomena and complex human intervention. It results from the accidental or artificial introduction of a foreign body inside the oyster. In response to this intrusion, the mantle, the animal's secretory organ, produces nacreous material to isolate the foreign body. The nucleus is gradually covered in nacre (mother-of-pearl).

The pearl farmer's job is to reproduce this mechanism methodically and on a large scale. The main operation is the grafting. A recipient oyster is fixed to a support and held open. Using a scalpel, the grafter incises the back of the gonad (reproductive organ) and inserts a minute particle of mantle removed from another oyster. The pearl farmer then introduces a perfectly spherical bead (the nucleus), about 6mm in diameter, into the gonad so that it is in contact with the graft. The operation takes a few seconds. The grafted oysters are placed inside metal baskets suspended from strings and lowered back into the lagoon. They are then regularly inspected and cleaned. Layer upon layer, the mother-of-pearl thickens around the nucleus at a rate of 1mm a year. Eighteen months later, the first harvest is gathered.

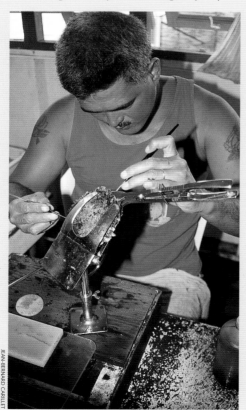

JEAN-BERNARD CARILLET

The pearls are used mainly for jewelry in rings and pendants. The factors determining their value are the diameter (from 8.5 to 18mm), shape, quality and color. "Black pearl" is in fact an inaccurate term. The pearl produced by *Pinctada margaritifera* covers a wide range of colors from pearly white to black, including deep purple, champagne and gray. The orient (the pearl's luster) and mirror effect are also taken into consideration.

A pearl farm employs numerous professional divers to take care of the underwater facilities. In Fakarava, you may have occasion to dive the farm in the breeding zone. The suspended baskets with hundreds of oysters look like necklaces and are photogenic. Ask the local dive center to arrange such a trip.

In Papeete, visit the Pearl Museum in the Vaima Center for more information on the pearling process.

39 La Faille

La Faille is a safe and comfortable dive that attracts all levels of divers. It has an interesting topography, abundant marine life and boasts excellent visibility that delights photographers. Topographically, it features a large fissure that carves the outside part of the reef north of the pass. The boat moors on the reeftop, where the water is 3m deep. Divers descend directly into the opening to explore the nooks and crannies.

Look for scorpionfish and moray eels. Fish feeding in Manihi usually takes place at this site. The prospect of a free meal generally attracts grey reef sharks and whitetip sharks as well as countless groupers, snappers, trevallies, Napoleon

Location: Southwest of the atoll

Depth Range: 15-25m (49-82ft)

Access: Boat

Expertise Rating: Novice

wrasse and triggerfish. After mealtime you then swim along the sheer drop-off, to the north and south of the break, between 15 and 25m. You finish the dive on the flat reeftop, where attractive coral formations provide an ideal habitat for small species, particularly shoals of black-striped surgeonfish.

PHILIPPE BACCHET

Look amid the countless crevices and boulders for moray eels, scorpionfish and surgeonfish.

Fakarava Dive Sites

Fakarava is another gigantic atoll, almost the same size as Rangiroa. Roughly rectangular in shape, its lagoon is 60km (37 miles) long and 25km (16 miles) wide. Unlike Rangiroa, Fakarava has little tourist infrastructure and retains a real sense of wilderness. It's the Tuamotus at their best. If you want a true atoll experience and to get away from it all, choose Fakarava. You'll feel like a pioneer.

The sites are totally untouched, and visibility is often exceptional. There are two dive areas: Garuae Pass, at the north end of the atoll, and Tumakohua Pass, at the south end of it—a 60km (37 miles) trip, which involves planning. At more than 800m wide, Garuae Pass is French Polynesia's largest. This monster is the meeting place for all sorts of deep-sea marine life. It is truly impressive. The Tumakohua

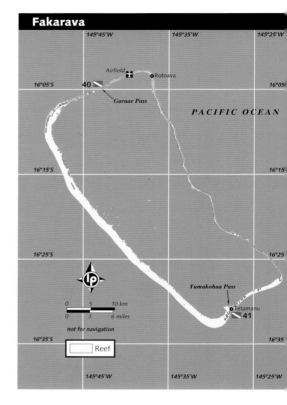

Fakarava

PACIFIC OCEAN

Have a picnic ashore on one of Fakarava's remote, unspoiled islets.

Pass is much smaller and offers less-challenging conditions, but it also boasts prolific marine life, both pelagics and reef species. In July, marbled groupers gather in massive shoals to breed. In Fakarava, more than anywhere else, you will know after your first dive what "moana"—the deep, intense blue—means.

The diving follows the same pattern as in Rangiroa and Manihi. Most dives are drift dives in an incoming current. Entry takes place in the ocean, and divers swim toward the pass in the deep blue before letting themselves be carried by the current into the lagoon. When the tide is going out, dives are made along the outer reef, away from the current. Experienced divers will enjoy these dives, but there are also a couple of dive sites suitable for novices. Certainly experience with currents is a great help.

What also distinguishes Fakarava from other atolls is the quality of the coral, which is an added charm to the dives. You will find vast expanses of *Montipora*, *Pocillopora* and *Acropora*.

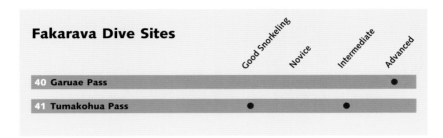

Fakarava Dive Sites

	Good Snorkeling	Novice	Intermediate	Advanced
40 Garuae Pass				●
41 Tumakohua Pass		●	●	

40 Garuae Pass

Without a doubt, this is the most sensational, thrill-packed dive in French Polynesia. It boasts all the characteristics of an exceptional site: impressive topography, an enormous variety of reef fish as well as pelagics, incredible dive conditions and a true sense of wilderness that is so typical of Fakarava atoll. Still seldom dived, it offers a pristine environment.

This gigantic pass, more than 800m wide, is the largest in French Polynesia. If you have just come from Rangiroa, Avatoru Pass and Tiputa Pass will seem like timid playgrounds in comparison. When the boat drops you at the ocean side of the pass, you'll have the impression that "anything can happen."

Location: North side of the atoll

Depth Range: 15-40m (49-131ft)

Access: Boat

Expertise Rating: Advanced

Swimming through an intense cobalt-blue void toward the entrance of the pass, you will be overwhelmed by the sight of the reef looming and plunging dramatically to abyssal depths. The powerful incoming current will then propel you into the channel, where the average depth is about 15m. Just let yourself be carried away, accompanied by a procession of swarming reef fish in the thousands.

You'll come across dozens of big, inquisitive sharks of many species—greys, whitetips, blacktips and probably massive silvertips—that congregate in the pass to hunt. Hammerheads, manta rays and big tuna can also be expected in the blue waters off the pass. Unlike Rangiroa's passes, the coral is excellent, with good growth on the pass bed. The boat collects you in the lagoon.

When the tide is going out, the dive is made outside the reef, along the reef rim and away from the current—the strong turbulence at the exit of the pass makes it extremely dangerous. In July, huge shoals of marbled groupers congregate here to breed. Approaching the outgoing tidal flow, you will see all the predators going to and fro in search of prey. Garuae Pass is definitely a fascinating dive.

FRÉDÉRIC DI MEGLIO

Thousands of fish funnel through Garuae Pass.

41　Tumakohua Pass

In contrast to the northern pass, Tumakohua Pass is much more relaxing, though it still retains that special wild flavor that typifies the diving in Fakarava. It is on a much more human scale, and the dive conditions are easier to handle.

The usual dive plan is a drift dive with the incoming current. You start in the open sea and swim toward the mouth of the pass, at about 30m. At the entrance of the pass, you'll see a wealth of small and large reef fish, including unicornfish, bigeyes, marbled groupers (they breed here in July), Napoleon wrasse, tuna, Forster's seapikes, trevallies, damselfish,

Location: South of the atoll

Depth Range: 15-40m (49-131ft)

Access: Boat

Expertise Rating: Intermediate

Moorish idols, triggerfish and angelfish, among others. The visibility is often superb and the current manageable enough to allow you to take your camera.

The pass bed gently ascends to a ridge at 15m, then slopes down again into the lagoon to about 30m. After passing the ridge, you continue down to a pleasant cave at 28m, carved in the right side of the pass and swarming with soldierfish. It forms an ideal perch from which to spot the horde of grey reef sharks that persistently prowl the vicinity. The pass bed is carpeted with excellent hard-coral outcrops that attract numerous reef fish.

An added charm to the dive is the series of long, white sand canyons dissecting the coral bed that look just like ski slopes. Whitetip sharks usually lie in these sandy gullies. The dive finishes literally at the foot of the stilt restaurant at the Tetamanu Village guest house, where schools of goatfish and snappers swarm among the coral formations—a perfect area for snorkeling.

When the tide is going out, you must stay safely outside the reef, along the reef rim and away from the current. There is a magnificent field of *Montipora* that mantles the reef from 35m downward, worth exploring if you are an experienced diver.

FREDERIC DI MEGLIO

The dive at Tumakohua Pass finishes in the shallows among schools of yellowfin goatfish.

Five hundred kilometers (300 miles) from the closest of the Tuamotus atolls, and 1400km (900) northeast of Papeete, the Marquesas are the most northerly archipelago of French Polynesia. The archipelago is made up of 15 islands, only six of which are inhabited. Unlike the high Society Islands, these islands have no sheltering reefs or lagoons.

Thus far, diving in the Marquesas is limited to the main island, Nuku Hiva. Diving in this region is unique, as the islands' topography is totally different from that found in the other archipelagoes.

The Marquesas don't boast coral reefs, peaceful lagoons or crystalline waters. The water is thick with plankton and rich in alluvium, and visibility is consequently reduced (generally 10 to 20m). One might think this is a drawback, but these specific conditions guarantee regular sightings of very unusual creatures, such as scalloped hammerheads and melon-headed whales, which are not encountered elsewhere in French Polynesia. All kinds of rays—mantas, eagles and stingrays—also swim close to the shore.

What also distinguishes the diving in the Marquesas is the abundance of caves. The cliffs are hollowed with numerous cavities that afford outstanding cave dives. There are around 10

JEAN-BERNARD CARILLET
Pelagic fish and mammals are drawn to the Marquesas.

established dive sites on the south and west coasts of Nuku Hiva. Since the Marquesan waters are devoid of any protective barrier reefs, divers should be prepared to cope with sometimes difficult conditions, particularly the swell, to get to the sites. Some sites require a half-hour or so boat trip.

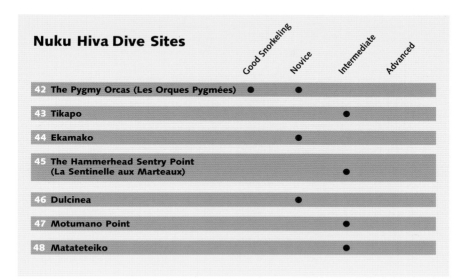

Nuku Hiva Dive Sites

	Good Snorkeling	Novice	Intermediate	Advanced
42 The Pygmy Orcas (Les Orques Pygmées)	●	●		
43 Tikapo			●	
44 Ekamako		●		
45 The Hammerhead Sentry Point (La Sentinelle aux Marteaux)			●	
46 Dulcinea		●		
47 Motumano Point			●	
48 Matateteiko			●	

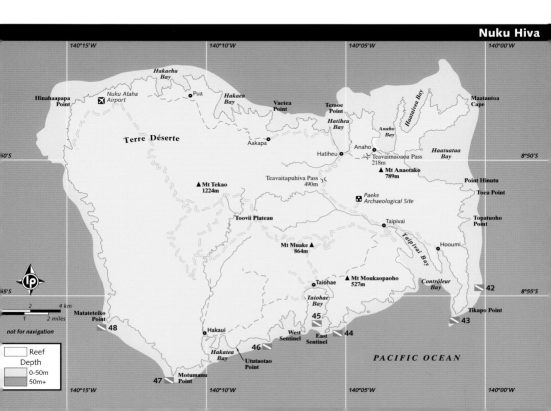

42   The Pygmy Orcas (Les Orques Pygmées)

This site is one of the most stunning in all of French Polynesia, though its location—off the east coast of Nuku Hiva—requires a tedious 35-minute boat trip from the town of Taiohae. Please note that good weather conditions are essential, as this side of the island is exposed to the prevailing winds and the swell. If the sea is choppy, it's not accessible. The November to March period is the calmest.

Location: East of Nuku Hiva

Depth Range: 1-10m (3-33ft)

Access: Boat

Expertise Rating: Novice

The prominent—and unique—feature of the dive is the incredible concentration of melon-headed whales (*Peponocephala electra*) that congregate in the area every morning. It's hard to count them, but according to some estimates, there can be as many as 400. They usually gather and stay at the surface, with their noses emerging, vertical or horizontal, sometimes playing, sometimes motionless. Snorkeling is the best way to approach them. You can hear their distinct, piercing sounds, and you will easily notice their white lips, which are thought to be phosphorescent at night to lure the squid they feed on. Though their habits are still largely unknown, some experts think that the east coast is their resting area during the day and that they go back to the west coast at night to feed. They usually make their appearance when the boat runs past Tikapo Point. It is a paradise for photographers, who may prefer to dive rather than snorkel so as to maximize their chances of getting the best shots.

The site itself is quite impressive, since it is anywhere between 300m and 1km off the coast, in a deep blue sea. Occasionally, one can also see yellowfin tuna and sailfish cruising through the area.

Snorkeling with melon-headed whales is a highlight of a visit to Nuku Hiva.

FREDERIC DI MEGLIO

43 Tikapo

This site boasts a spectacular topography. Rising from the depths, a rocky peak brushes the surface, approximately 400m south of Tikapo Point, which extends like a finger pointing into the ocean at the southeastern tip of the island. Its isolation, combined with the deep water in which it lies, makes Tikapo a perfect place for spotting a dense population of both pelagic and reef species.

Location: Southeast of Nuku Hiva

Depth Range: 10-35m (33-115ft)

Access: Boat

Expertise Rating: Intermediate

The main drawback is the rather forceful prevailing north-south current, making Tikapo unsuitable for novice divers. Photographers will enjoy this site, particularly for shooting pelagics, as the current is too tricky to master close-ups of smaller fish.

On a typical dive plan, the boat shelters in Taipivai Bay, five minutes away, to avoid an uncomfortable pre-dive briefing and equipment preparation.

The peak features two different profiles. On the western side, it steps down gently to 30 to 35m, offering three plateaus at 10m, 20 to 25m and 30 to 35m. The eastern side is a sheer drop to a plateau at 25m, the edge of which overlooks the blue and is the ideal place for sighting eagle rays and the occasional mantas. Some sections of the rock between 18 and 20m are peppered with caverns. Going around the peak, you will come upon impressive schools of trevallies, unicornfish and barracuda sweeping around in search of easy pickings. There are large numbers of parrotfish, triggerfish, butterflyfish, pufferfish, soldierfish and hunting packs of tuna, together with scorpionfish around the crevices. Whitetip reef sharks are also common here. Invertebrates are relatively limited, except for porcelain crabs, urchins and encrusting sponges that form delicate orange patches.

44 Ekamako

Close to the eastern exit of Taiohae Bay, this site offers an unforgettable cave diving experience and provides a unique opportunity to approach stingrays. It centers on a large, open-fronted cavern deeply undercutting the basaltic cliff at 10m. A flashlight is indispensable for exploring the cavern.

Location: East of Taiohae Bay, south of the island

Depth Range: 8-10m (26-33ft)

Access: Boat

Expertise Rating: Novice

The entrance to the cave is sufficiently wide and high, as is the interior, making it suitable for novice divers. Upon entering, you will cross a vast chamber that continues on the right until a freshwater resurgence; on the left, it slopes up smoothly to an air pocket. The sandy bottoms of both sections are literally carpeted by big stingrays, the star attraction of the dive. Partially hidden in the sand, they have found the perfect conditions to rest and probably to breed. Pay careful attention to buoyancy so as not to stir up silt, and be careful not to kick an animal with your fins. If you swim gently above them, they may not even move. Some, scared by the lights and the presence of divers, swim away. The numerous crevices and fissures in the left section of the cave are home to huge lobsters. Given the shallow depth, you will have plenty of time to explore all the nooks and crannies of the cave.

Bring your dive light to spot Ekamako's resident stingrays.

45 The Hammerhead Sentry Point (La Sentinelle aux Marteaux)

The strong point of this appropriately named dive is the high probability of seeing schools of scalloped hammerhead sharks, and occasionally manta rays. According to statistics compiled by the local dive operator, divers have a 75% chance of spotting hammerheads during their dive. The site is at the exact eastern corner of the exit of Taiohae Bay.

Location: Exit of Taiohae Bay

Depth Range: 10-30m (33-98ft)

Access: Boat

Expertise Rating: Intermediate

The underwater topography echoes the steep basalt cliffs. It plunges to a sandy bottom at 50m, and the dive mainly consists of swimming along the drop-off at depths ranging from 10 to 30m, according to activity. Usually the sharks pass by at a depth of less than 15m, which provides a unique opportunity for novice divers to approach them in shallow waters. The sharks are often curious and will come close to divers. At about 30m, the wall forms a small ledge.

The area at the entrance to the bay, more exposed to the swell, is rather choppy compared to the calm waters inside the bay. Visibility amounts to 15m on average, but can be reduced to 5m at low tide when the current, flowing out of the bay, carries particles. In this case, your chances of glimpsing the hammerheads dwindle dramatically. Manta rays occasionally patrol the site as well.

There is no convincing explanation for the concentration of hammerheads in the vicinity. According to local dive instructors, the turbid, plankton-filled waters that prevail here attract them, and females are known to give birth near the wharf inside the bay, not far from the site.

If sharks are not in the area or if the visibility is minimal, focus on the wall.

Its caverns form a good habitat for moray eels and scorpionfish, and shells are plentiful, including the *Gauguini*, a species endemic to the Marquesas that is ideal for macrophotography.

46 Dulcinea

Dulcinea consists of a rocky seamount brushing the surface in a protected bay west of Taiohae. It features an interesting underwater topography that is divided into two connected tunnels shaped like an inverted V. The smaller branch of the V forms the main entrance, at 10m, and leads to a number of large boulders with openings that allow beams of sunlight to pass through. You will then follow the second tunnel on your right, which gradually descends to the exit at 20m. The site is typically profuse with snappers, urchins, shells, lobsters and other crustaceans, together with curtains of soldierfish that provide a magnificent backdrop for photographers near the exit.

Novice divers wishing to experience cave diving will appreciate this site because the conditions are optimal. Though a flashlight is recommended, you

Location: West of Taiohae

Depth Range: 10-20m (33-66ft)

Access: Boat

Expertise Rating: Novice

never lose sight of natural light. Most of the way is large enough for several divers to swim through side-by-side, except for a tiny section in the second tunnel that is only 1.5m high but easily negotiated. There is no risk of stirring up silt and losing your visibility, since polished pebbles carpet the floor.

After exploring the cave, you can finish your dive swimming around the huge boulders in the area, where canyons and arches are plentiful.

FRÉDÉRIC DI MEGLIO

Legions of soldierfish patrol the tunnel openings at Dulcinea.

47 Motumano Point (Pointe Motumano)

Motumano lies at the southwestern tip of the island and refers to a rocky promontory that extends into the open sea. This strategic location, exposed to open-sea currents, acts as a magnet for pelagics. Numerous sharks, in particular hammerheads and whitetip reef sharks, have made this area their hunting ground. And if you want to approach manta rays, this is a site not to be missed.

The massive cliffs slide down under the water and form a gentle drop-off until a sandy area at 30 to 40m. The dive starts at the very bottom of the cliff, a relatively calm area protected from the surge and the prevailing winds. Swim first toward the west and then go south to reach the extremity of the tip. You'll pass many boulders scattered around that are worth exploring, as they sup-

Location: Southwest of Nuku Hiva

Depth Range: 15-40m (49-131ft)

Access: Boat

Expertise Rating: Intermediate

port a host of small reef fish. Be on the lookout for schools of snappers, barracuda, trevallies and the star attractions of the dive—eagle rays, manta rays and hammerheads. Whitetip reef sharks tend to gather around the extremity of the tip, an area subject to a surge and strong currents. To finish your dive, turn back toward the sheltered western side of the cliff, where the boat will pick you up.

Move slowly and you may be rewarded with a manta encounter.

FREDERIC DI MEGLIO

48 Matateteiko

At the western side of the island, this site is the farthest from Taiohae. It features a rocky platform visible from the surface at the bottom of the cliff that continues underwater for about 100m toward the open sea. Entry takes place in a sheltered inlet next to the emerging platform. The descent is gradual until 30m. It is bordered by walls and peppered with small canyons and caverns.

Location: West of Nuku Hiva

Depth Range: 15-30m (49-98ft)

Access: Boat

Expertise Rating: Intermediate

Follow the platform that extends perpendicular to the cliff until you reach a lip that overlooks a sheer wall. This point is an ideal location for admiring schools of prowling predators: barracuda, trevallies, tuna and sometimes whitetip reef sharks.

Expect a challenging current that usually sweeps over the area from south to east, but also expect the most prolific underwater life drifting with the turbulence. Then turn back and head toward the cliff and explore one of the walls that border the platform (though less exposed to current, the southern side is also less abundant in marine life).

Take the time to explore the small canyons and scattered boulders, as they harbor soldierfish, octopuses, lobsters and snappers. While inspecting all the nooks and crannies, be sure to look around and above you so as not to miss the manta rays and hammerheads that often pass by in the shallow waters near the cliff.

FRÉDÉRIC DI MEGLIO

Strong currents carry food for shoals of snappers.

Rurutu Dive Site

Well to the south of Tahiti and the Society Islands, the Austral Group runs north-west to southeast and is effectively an extension of the same range of submerged peaks that make up the Cook Islands. Rurutu is the main island of the Australs. It is about 10km (6 miles) long and averages 5km (3 miles) wide. The island is fringed by a continuous reef, but it is rarely more than a stone's throw from the shoreline. There is no lagoon. Limestone caverns dot the coast. Unlike the Society Islands, the Australs are not yet established as a tourist destination, and Rurutu is no exception, though there are several comfortable guest houses to accommodate those who want to experience a different, more genuine Polynesia.

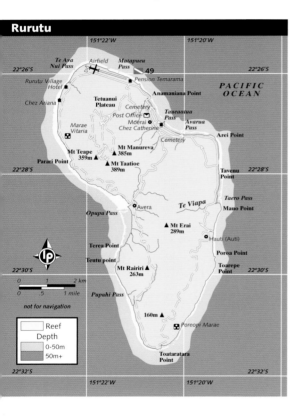

The highlight of diving in the Australs is the humpback whales that come to the area to reproduce, calve and nurse from July to October. The return migration to the colder Antarctic waters begins in late October. Unlike other popular whale-watching spots in the world, such as Hawaii or Alaska, whale watching in Rurutu has not reached such large-scale (or regulated) proportions, and snorkelers can get surprisingly close to these gentle giants. The island remains off the beaten track and offers a real sense of adventure to snorkelers, who may have the privilege to swim among groups of cooperative humpback whales.

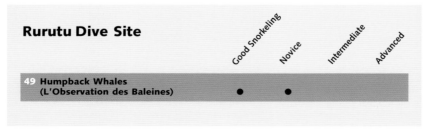

Rurutu Dive Site	Good Snorkeling	Novice	Intermediate	Advanced
49 Humpback Whales (L'Observation des Baleines)	●	●		

49 Humpback Whales (L'Observation des Baleines)

This might be the most unusual "site" in French Polynesia. It is not a specific dive site, but a huge area off the coast visited by humpback whales from July to October. Instead of scuba diving, you will snorkel.

Location: North of the island

Depth Range: 1-5m (3-16ft)

Access: Boat

Expertise Rating: Novice

Snorkeling with the whales is organized through Raie Manta Club Rurutu, an offshoot of the reputable Raie Manta Club in Rangiroa, Tuamotus. The divemaster has several years of experience and intimately understands the habits and behavior of the mammals. The boat usually leaves twice a day for a three-hour trip. It is important to note that cetacean encounters cannot be guaranteed at all times; they are common but unpredictable. To maximize your chances of seeing the mammals, a one-week stay is recommended.

Once the divemaster has located the whales, you will don your wetsuit, mask, fins and snorkel and follow carefully the instructions before entering the water. You will see the whales at the surface, spraying water from their blowholes, and may observe a full breach, when they propel up to two-thirds of their body out of the water. Underwater, the sight of these 10 to 15m long giants is indescribable. Depending on their mood, mother whales may come right up to the boat, showing off their new offspring, who can also be seen suckling. Free divers and snorkelers should take care not touch these animals or harass them in any way.

For photographers, this site is a must. You can get exceptional, once-in-a-lifetime images.

LIONEL POZZOLI

You, a snorkel and a 40-ton humpback whale—unforgettable!

FRÉDÉRIC DI MEGLIO

Marine Life

The marine life in French Polynesia is renowned for its abundance and diversity. You will find both the usual reef fish as well as numerous pelagics, with sharks being the star attraction. Coral growth here cannot compare with most areas of the Indian Ocean, although the hard coral can be excellent in places. Soft coral is not so widespread in French Polynesia. The listing below represents just a sampling of the great range of life found in this region.

Common names are used freely but are notoriously inaccurate and inconsistent. The two-part scientific name, usually shown in italics, is more precise. It consists of a genus name followed by a species name. A genus is a group of closely related species that share common features. A species is a recognizable group within a genus whose members are capable of interbreeding. Where the species or genus is unknown, the naming reverts to the next known level: family (F), order (O), class (C) or phylum (Ph).

Common Vertebrates

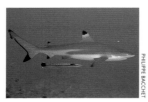
blacktip reef shark
Carcharhinus melanopterus

whitetip shark
Triaenodon obesus

silvertip shark
Carcharhinus albimarginatus

lemon shark
Negaprion acutidens

grey reef shark
Carcharhinus amblyrhynchos

manta ray
Manta birostris

120

eagle ray
Aetobatus narinari

black-striped surgeonfish
Acanthurus triostegus

bluefin trevally
Caranx melampygus

anemonefish
F. Pomacentridae

trumpetfish
Aulostomus chinensis

bluescale emperor
F. Lethrinidae

bluestripe snapper
Lutjanus kasmira

marbled grouper
Epinephelus polyphekadion

parrotfish
F. Scaridae

titan triggerfish
Balistoides viridescens

damselfish
F. Pomacentridae

peacock rockcod
Cephalopholis argus

long-jawed squirrelfish
Sargocentron spiniferum

Moorish idol
Zanclus cornutus

Pacific double-saddle butterflyfish
Chaetodon ulietensis

whitecheek surgeonfish
Acanthurus nigricans

Napoleon wrasse
Cheilinus undulatus

Forster's seapike
Sphyraena forsteri

Common Invertebrates

giant clam
Tridacna gigas

plate coral
Montipora sp.

branching coral
Pocillopora sp.

staghorn coral
Acropora sp.

cabbage coral
Turbinaria sp.

sea fans
F. Gorgonidae

chromodoris
F. Chromodorididae

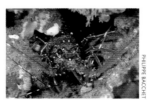

spiny lobster
F. Palinuridae

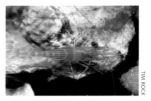

bigeye shrimp
F. Rhynchocinetidae

anemone
F. Stichodactylidae

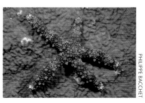

sea star
F. Ophidiasteridae

sea cucumber
F. Stichopodidae

Hazardous Marine Life

Marine creatures almost never attack divers, but many have defensive and offensive weaponry that can be triggered if they feel threatened or annoyed. The ability to recognize hazardous creatures is a valuable asset in avoiding accident and injury. The following are some of the potentially hazardous creatures most commonly found in French Polynesia.

Fire Coral

Although often mistaken for stony coral, fire coral is a hydroid colony that secretes a hard, calcareous skeleton. Fire coral grows in many different shapes, often encrusting or taking the form of a variety of reef structures. It is usually identifiable by its tan, mustard or brown color and finger-like columns with whitish tips. The entire colony is covered by tiny pores and fine, hair-like projections nearly invisible to the unaided eye. Fire coral "stings" by discharging small, specialized cells called nematocysts. Contact causes a burning sensation that lasts for several minutes and may produce red welts on the skin. Do not rub the area, as you will only spread the stinging particles. Cortisone cream can reduce the inflammation, and antihistamine cream is good for killing the pain. Serious stings should be treated by a doctor.

Cone Shell

Do not touch or pick up cone shells. These mollusks deliver a venomous sting by shooting a tiny poison dart from their funnel-like proboscis. Stings will cause numbness and can be followed by muscular paralysis or even respiratory paralysis and heart failure. Immobilize the victim, apply a pressure bandage, be prepared to use CPR, and seek urgent medical aid.

PHILIPPE BACCHET

PHILIPPE BACCHET
Stonefish are particularly difficult to spot.

Scorpionfish & Stonefish

Scorpionfish and stonefish are well-camouflaged creatures that have poisonous spines along their dorsal fins. They are often difficult to spot since they typically rest quietly on the bottom or on coral, looking more like rocks. Practice good buoyancy control and watch where you put your hands. Scorpionfish and stonefish wounds can be excruciating. To treat a puncture, wash the wound and immerse in nonscalding hot water for 30 to 90 minutes. Administer pain medications and seek medical aid if necessary.

Moray Eel

Distinguished by their long, thick, snake-like bodies and tapered heads, moray eels come in a variety of colors and patterns. Don't feed them or put your hand in a dark hole—eels have the unfortunate combination of sharp teeth and poor eyesight, and will bite if they feel threatened. If you are bitten, don't try to pull your hand away suddenly—the teeth slant backward and are extraordinarily sharp. Let the eel release it and then surface slowly. Treat with antiseptics, antitetanus and antibiotics.

PHILIPPE BACCHET

Stingray

Identified by its diamond-shaped body and wide "wings," the stingray has one or two venomous spines at the base of its tail. Stingrays like shallow waters and tend to rest on silty or sandy bottoms, often burying themselves in the sand. Often

PHILIPPE BACCHET

only the eyes, gill slits and tail are visible. These creatures are harmless unless you sit or step on them. Though injuries are uncommon, wounds are always extremely painful, and often deep and infective. Immerse wound in nonscalding hot water, administer pain medications and seek medical aid.

Barracuda

Barracuda are identifiable by their long, silver, cylindrical bodies and razor-like teeth protruding from an underslung jaw. They swim alone or in small groups, continually opening and closing their mouths, an action that looks daunting, but actually assists their respiration. Though barracuda will hover near divers to observe, they are really somewhat shy, though they may be attracted by shiny objects that resemble fishing lures. Irrigate a barracuda bite with fresh water and treat with antiseptics, anti-tetanus and antibiotics.

Lionfish

Also known as turkeyfish or firefish, these slow, graceful fish extend their feathery pectoral fins as they swim. They have distinctive vertical brown or black bands alternating with narrower pink or white bands. When threatened or provoked, lionfish may inject venom through dorsal spines that can penetrate booties, wetsuits and leather gloves. The wounds can be extremely painful. If you're stung, wash the wound and immerse in non-scalding hot water for 30 to 90 minutes.

Shark

In Tahiti, the most common species of sharks are the silvertip reef, the blacktip reef, the whitetip reef, the grey reef, the lemon and the hammerhead. Sharks are most recognizable by their triangular dorsal fin. Though many species are shy, there are occasional attacks. Sharks will generally not attack unless provoked, so don't taunt or tease them. The only reported shark attacks in French Polynesia have been against spearfishers carrying dead or wounded fish at the belt. Face and quietly watch any shark that is acting aggressively and be prepared to push it away with camera, knife or tank. If someone is bitten by a shark, stop the bleeding, reassure the patient, treat for shock and seek immediate medical aid.

Diving Conservation & Awareness

JEAN-BERNARD CARILLET

Though French Polynesia epitomizes paradise on earth, lingering environmental problems tarnish this reputation. Atolls and high islands are ecologically vulnerable, and French Polynesia has been slow in implementing protective regulations.

Garbage is certainly a less appealing aspect. It's not unusual to see garbage dumps despoiling the natural setting, even next to a lagoon, and inhabitants and visitors still toss cans and bottles into the lagoon. On land, garbage pollutes watercourses, which in turn pollute the lagoons. The sewage stations, when they exist, are poorly maintained, resulting in badly treated outflow that ends up in the sea. Coral reefs are especially at stake, and the situation is a particular concern in urban areas of Tahiti and the other Leeward Islands.

Another type of human impact arises from overfishing, particularly in the Society Islands and in the Tuamotus, where big fish traps are set in the passes to atoll lagoons. The pearl industry exerts another environmental pressure. Some of the lagoons in the Tuamotus support up to 70 pearl farms, and the runoff from these farms pollutes the surrounding water.

There are a few marine reserves in French Polynesia, including Scilly and Bellinghausen in the Society Islands and Taiaro in the Tuamotus, along with some protected areas, including Eiao, in the Marquesas. In Rangiroa, there are plans to preserve Blue Lagoon, Les Sables Roses and L'Île aux Récifs.

Turtles and rays are officially protected, and may not be harmed. There are size and seasonal limits for other species of fish and crustaceans, including lobsters. Whether these measures are actually enforced is another matter. Turtles continue to be poached for their flesh and their shells, which are used as ornaments.

Other natural and manmade threats to the reef include coral bleaching, cyclones and bad anchoring practices. It is estimated that coral bleaching has killed between 20 and 50% of corals in the last 20 years. Though uncommon, cyclones take their toll as well and seriously damage the upper part of the reef. The reef is also damaged by indiscriminate boat anchoring. Only a few dive sites have mooring buoys, resulting in anchoring practices that can damage the fragile reef life.

Although French underwater nuclear testing was halted in 1995, the effects of almost 30 years of such testing are only starting to be understood. In 1999 the French government admitted for the first time that the coral cones at the site of the tests, Moruroa Atoll, were fissured and that radioactivity had escaped. Other possible effects of the testing are not known.

Responsible Diving

Dive sites tend to be located where the reefs and walls display the most beautiful corals and sponges. It only takes a moment—an inadvertently placed hand or knee, or a careless brush or kick with a fin—to destroy this fragile, living part of our delicate ecosystem. By following certain basic guidelines while diving, you can help preserve the ecology and beauty of the reefs:

1. Never drop boat anchors onto a coral reef and take care not to ground boats on coral. Encourage dive operators and regulatory bodies in their efforts to establish permanent moorings at appropriate dive sites.

2. Practice and maintain proper buoyancy control and avoid over-weighting. Be aware that buoyancy can change over the period of an extended trip. Initially you may breathe harder and need more weighting; a few days later you may breathe more easily and need less weight. Tip: Use your weight belt and tank position to maintain a horizontal position—raise them to elevate your feet, lower them to elevate your upper body. Also be careful about buoyancy loss: as you go deeper, your wetsuit compresses, as does the air in your BC.

3. Avoid touching living marine organisms with your body and equipment. Polyps can be damaged by even the gentlest contact. Never stand on or touch living coral. The use of gloves is no longer recommended: gloves make it too easy to hold on to the reef. The abrasion caused by gloves may be even more damaging to the reef than your hands are. If you must hold on to the reef, touch only exposed rock or dead coral.

4. Take great care in underwater caves. Spend as little time within them as possible, as your air bubbles can damage fragile

PHILIPPE BACCHET

Try not to disturb marine life—let them approach you.

organisms. Divers should take turns inspecting the interiors of small caves or under ledges to lessen the chances of damaging contact.

5. Be conscious of your fins. Even without contact, the surge from heavy fin strokes near the reef can do damage. Avoid full-leg kicks when diving close to the bottom and when leaving a photo scene. When you inadvertently kick something, stop kicking! It seems obvious, but some divers either panic or are totally oblivious when they bump something. When treading water in shallow reef areas, take care not to kick up clouds of sand. Settling sand can smother the delicate reef organisms.

6. Secure gauges, computer consoles and the octopus regulator so they're not dangling—they are like miniature wrecking balls to a reef.

7. When swimming in strong currents, be extra careful about leg kicks and handholds.

8. Photographers should take extra precautions, as cameras and equipment affect buoyancy. Changing f-stops, framing a subject and maintaining position for a photo often conspire to prohibit the ideal "no-touch" approach on a reef. When you must use "holdfasts," choose them intelligently (i.e., use one finger only for leverage off an area of dead coral).

9. Resist the temptation to collect or buy coral or shells. Aside from the ecological damage, taking home marine souvenirs depletes the beauty of a site and spoils other divers' enjoyment.

10. Ensure that you take home all your trash and any litter you may find as well. Plastics in particular pose a serious threat to marine life.

11. Resist the temptation to feed fish. You may disturb their normal eating habits, encourage aggressive behavior or feed them food that is detrimental to their health.

12. Minimize your disturbance of marine animals. Don't ride on the backs of turtles or manta rays, as this can cause them great anxiety.

Marine Conservation Organizations

The following groups are actively involved in promoting responsible diving practices, publicizing environmental marine threats and lobbying for better policies:

CORAL: The Coral Reef Alliance
☎ 510-848-0110
www.coral.org

Ocean Futures
☎ 805-899-8899
www.oceanfutures.com

Cousteau Society
☎ 757-523-9335
www.cousteau.org

ReefKeeper International
☎ 305-358-4600
www.reefkeeper.org

Project AWARE Foundation
☎ 714-540-0251
www.projectaware.org

Listings

Telephone Calls

To call French Polynesia, dial the international access code for the country you are calling from, + 689 (French Polynesia's country code) + the six-digit local number.

Diving Services

There are approximately 25 dive centers in French Polynesia. The centers are affiliated with a number of dive associations, including the French FFESSM (affiliated with CMAS), PADI and SSI. The staff usually speak English. They are open year-round, most of them every day. Gear rental is usually included in the price of the dive.

All types of courses—PADI and CMAS—and dives are available. The centers typically offer two to three dives a day, generally at 8 or 9am and around 2pm. All centers have at least one boat. Most centers do not have a definite schedule for dives but decide each day which sites are most suitable for the weather conditions. It's a good idea to reserve at least a day in advance. Almost all of them accept credit cards, and many videotape dives. Most (except for those on Tahiti) offer free pick-ups within a certain area.

Tahiti

Aquatica Dive Center
P.O. Box 380 554
Tamanu
98718 Punaaiua
Tahiti, French Polynesia
☎ 53 34 96 fax: 43 10 65
aquatica_dive@hotmail.com
www.tahiti-resorts.com/aquatica.htm
Other: Based in Beachcomber Parkroyal Hotel, km 8

Eleuthera Plongee
P.O. Box 13029
Punaaiua
Tahiti, French Polynesia
☎ 42 49 29 fax: 43 66 22
eleut@tahiti-dive.pf
www.tahiti-dive.pf
Other: Based in marina Taina, km 9

Iti Diving International
P.O. Box 7540

98719 Taravao
Tahiti, French Polynesia
☎/fax: 57 77 93
itidiving@hotmail.com
Other: Based in marina Puunui, on Tahiti Iti

Nautisports
Fare Ute district
P.O. Box 62 Papeete
Tahiti, French Polynesia
☎ 50 59 59
Other: Dive equipment sales

Ocean World
P.O. Box 380 595
Tamanu
98718 Punaaiua
Tahiti, French Polynesia
☎/fax: 45 21 98
oceanworld@mail.pf
Other: Based in Hotel Le Meridien, km 15

Tahiti (continued)

Scubatek Tahiti
P.O. Box 1456 Papeete
Tahiti, French Polynesia
☎/fax: 42 23 55
plc.scubatek@mail.pf
Other: In Arue yacht club, km 4; nitrox
dives available

Tahiti Plongee
P.O. Box 2192 Papeete
Tahiti, French Polynesia
☎ 41 00 62 fax: 42 26 06
Other: Based in Punaaiua, km 7.5; special
courses for children; rents and sells dive
equipment

Moorea

Bathy's Club
P.O. Box 1247 Papetoai
98729 Moorea
French Polynesia
☎ 56 31 44, 55 19 39 fax: 56 38 10
bathys@mail.pf
Other: Based in Beachcomber Parkroyal
Hotel, km 28

Moorea Fun Dive
P.O. Box 737 Maharepa
98728 Moorea
French Polynesia
☎ 56 40 38, 56 40 74 fax: 56 40 74
fundive@mail.pf
www.fundive.pf
Other: Based in Moora Beach Club, km 26

M.U.S.T.
P.O. Box 336
Moorea, French Polynesia
☎ 56 17 32 fax: 56 15 83
mustdive@mail.pf
www.tahiti-
explorer.com/dive_moorea.html
Other: Based in Cook's Bay

Scubapiti
P.O. Box 563 Maharepa
Moorea, French Polynesia
☎/fax: 56 20 38
Other: Based in Les Tipaniers Hotel, km
25; the only dive center on Moorea that
does not offer shark and fish feeding

Huahine

Centre Nautique Oiri
P.O. Box 39 Fare
Huahine, French Polynesia
☎/fax: 68 76 84
Other: Based in Huahine Beach Club,
Parea (south of the island)

Pacific Blue Adventure
P.O. Box 193 Fare
Huahine, French Polynesia
☎ 68 87 21 fax: 68 80 71
Other: Based in Fare, north of the island

Raiatea

Hemisphere Sub
P.O. Box 985
98735 Uturoa
Raiatea, French Polynesia

☎ 66 12 49 fax: 66 28 63
hemis-subdiving@mail.pf
Other: Based in marina Apooiti

Bora Bora

Bora Bora Blue Nui
Bora Bora, French Polynesia
☎ 67 79 07 or ☎ 96 42 73 fax: 67 79 07
boraborabluenui@mail.pf
Other: Based in Bora Bora Pearl Beach
Resort

Bora Diving Center
P.O. Box 182 Vaitape
Bora Bora, French Polynesia
☎ 67 71 84 fax: 67 74 83
boradiving@mail.pf
Other: Based in Matira Point

Bora Bora (continued)

Nemo World
P.O. Box 503 Vaitape
Bora Bora, French Polynesia
☎ 67 77 85 fax: 67 63 33
divebora@mail.pf
Other: Based in Matira Point

Topdive
P.O. Box 515 Vaitape
Bora Bora, French Polynesia
☎ 60 50 50 fax: 60 50 51
olivier@topdive.pf
www.topdive.com

Rangiroa

Raie Manta Club
P.O. Box 55 Avatoru
98775 Rangiroa
French Polynesia
☎ 96 84 80 fax: 96 85 60

The Six Passengers
P.O. Box 128 Avatoru
98775 Rangiroa
French Polynesia

☎ 96 03 05 fax: 96 02 60
the6passengers@mail.pf
www.emoc.com/sixpassengers

Paradive
P.O. Box 75 Avatoru
Rangiroa, Tuamotu
French Polynesia
☎ 96 05 55 fax: 96 05 50

Manihi

Manihi Blue Nui
Manihi, Tuamotu
French Polynesia
☎/fax: 96 42 17

Mahihi.Blue.Nui@mail.pf
Other: Based in the Manihi Pearl Beach
Resort

Fakarava

Te Ava Nui
P.O. Box 500 Rotoava
98763 Fakarava

French Polynesia
☎/fax: 98 42 50

Nuku Hiva

Centre Plongee Marquises
P.O. Box 100 Taiohae
Nuku Hiva, Marquesas

French Polynesia
☎/fax: 92 00 88
Other: Based in Taiohae

Rurutu

Raie Manta Club Rurutu
Rurutu Village
P.O. Box 22 Moerai
98753 Rurutu

Australs, French Polynesia
☎ 96 84 80 fax: 96 85 60 (in Rangiroa)
Other: Open from July to October

Live-Aboards

Archipels Croisières
P.O. Box 1160 Papetoai
Moorea, French Polynesia
☎ 56 36 39 fax: 56 35 87
archimoo@mail.pf
www.archipels.com
Home port: Rangiroa (Tuamotu) or
Nuku Hiva (Marquesas)
Description: 17.5m catamaran
Passengers: 8
Destinations: Rangiroa, all islands of the
Marquesas archipelago
Duration: 3-8 days
Season: Year-round

Aqua Polynésie
P.O. Box 4500 Papeete
Tahiti, French Polynesia
☎/fax: 85 00 00
Home port: Fakarava, Bora Bora or
Nuku Hiva
Description: 14m catamaran

Passengers: 6
Destinations: Leeward Islands: Tuamotus
(Fakarava and nearby atolls); Marquesas
(Nuku Hiva, Ua Huka, Ua Pou)
Duration: 8 days
Season: Year-round (Tuamotus); March to
Nov. (Leeward Islands); Dec. to Feb.
(Marquesas)

VPM Dufour Yachting
P.O. Box 554 Maharepa
Moorea, French Polynesia
☎ 56 40 50 fax: 56 40 60
vpm@nouvelles-frontieres.fr
Home port: Fakarava
Description: 25m catamaran
Passengers: 12
Destinations: Tuamotus (Fakarava and
nearby atolls)
Duration: 12 days
Season: Year-round

Tourist Offices

The helpful Tahiti Tourisme offers a wealth of free information about each tourist
island. Resources include up-to-date brochures on accommodations (from guesthouses to luxury resorts), activities, transportation, a calendar of events and more.
Check their website for more information: www.tahiti-tourisme.com.

In Papeete, Tahiti Tourisme is conveniently located on the waterfront side of Blvd
Pomare, close to the cruise ship quay, across from rue Paul-Gauguin in the center.

> **Tahiti Tourisme**
> P.O. Box 65 Papeete
> Tahiti, French Polynesia
> tahiti-tourisme@mail.pf

Tahiti Tourisme overseas representatives include:

Australia
The Limerick Castle
12 Ann St,
Surry Hills NSW 2010
☎ 2 92 81 6020 fax: 2 9211 6589
paramor@ozemail.com.au

France
28, Blvd Saint-Germain
75005 Paris
☎ 01 55 42 61 21 fax 01 55 42 61 20
tahitipar@calva.net

Germany
Bockenheimer, Landstr 45
D-60 325
Frankfurt/Main
☎ 69-9714 84 fax 7292 75

U.S.A.
300 Continental Blvd, Suite 160
El Segundo, California 90245
☎ 310-414-8484 fax: 310-414-8490
tahitilax@earthlink.net
www.gototahiti.com

Index

dive sites covered in this book appear in **bold** type

Lonely Planet Pisces Books

The **Diving & Snorkeling** guides cover top destinations worldwide. Beautifully illustrated with full-color photos throughout, the series explores the best diving and snorkeling areas and prepares divers for what to expect when they get there. Each site is described in detail, with information on suggested ability levels, depth, visibility and, of course, marine life. There's basic topside information as well for each destination.

Also check out dive guides to:

Australia: Southeast Coast	Bonaire	Monterey Peninsula & Northern California	Scotland
Baja California	British Virgin Islands	Pacific Northwest	Seychelles
Bahamas: Family Islands & Grand Bahama	Cocos Island	Puerto Rico	Southern California
Bahamas: Nassau & New Providence	Curaçao	Red Sea	Texas
Bali & Lombok	Dominica	Roatan & Honduras' Bay Islands	Trinidad & Tobago
Bermuda	Florida Keys		Turks & Caicos
	Jamaica		Vanuatu

Lonely Planet Publications

Australia
Locked Bag 1, Footscray, Victoria, 3011
☎ (03) 9689 4666 fax: (03) 9689 6833
email: talk2us@lonelyplanet.com.au

USA
150 Linden Street
Oakland, California 94607
☎ (510) 893 8555, (800) 275 8555
fax: (510) 893 8563
email: info@lonelyplanet.com

UK
10a Spring Place,
London NW5 3BH
☎ (0171) 428 4800 fax: (0171) 428 4828
email: go@lonelyplanet.co.uk

France
1 rue du Dahomey
75011 Paris
☎ 01 55 25 33 00 fax: 01 55 25 33 01
email: bip@lonelyplanet.fr

www.lonelyplanet.com